AMERICAN PRISONER OF WAR CAMPS
IN WASHINGTON AND OREGON

KATHY KIRKPATRICK

AMERICA
THROUGH TIME®
ADDING COLOR TO AMERICAN HISTORY

For Carmelina

America Through Time is an imprint of Fonthill Media LLC
www.through-time.com
office@through-time.com

Published by Arcadia Publishing by arrangement with Fonthill Media LLC
For all general information, please contact Arcadia Publishing:

Telephone: 843-853-2070
Fax: 843-853-0044
E-mail: sales@arcadiapublishing.com
For customer service and orders:
Toll-Free 1-888-313-2665

www.arcadiapublishing.com

First published 2019

Copyright © Kathy Kirkpatrick 2019

ISBN 978-1-63499-150-6

Typeset in Minion Pro 10pt on 13pt
Printed and bound in England

Contents

List of Illustrations

Introduction

America is a nation of immigrants, so hosting prisoners of war (POWs) from their home-lands brought mixed feelings among the civilians and military in the communities where the prisoners were housed and worked. For many farmers who had immigrated to the Midwest, being able to contract for German POW labor not only eased the labor shortage, but it also brought the opportunity to speak their native language, perhaps to learn about family and friends left behind when they moved to America. It also often gave them the opportunity to provide additional food for men who worked hard for them and shared their friendship. Although these Americans had sons fighting in the war, they were more aware of the lack of choices these German prisoners had in their own lives than those who had not left an oppressive homeland.

The same situation applied to Italian immigrants and Italian POWs with the additional benefit of a less strained relationship after Italy became a part of the Allied cause in September 1943. The resulting friendships (and some marriages) show the very positive results of their experiences under very difficult circumstances.

In fact, when German-American or Italian-American families were given permission to hire prisoners of war to work on their farms or canneries, they were being given a measure of approval often missing in their own communities. In 1940, 330,000 Germans and 694,000 Italians had registered as aliens. Those not living on the coasts were not displaced but suffered the name-calling and ostracism promoted by the government and media directed at those groups of people during that time to promote the war effort. They could be arrested just for translating English into German for an aged grandparent.

The stories shared in the course of researching this topic include a moving description by a young Girl Scout raising the flag while a truck load of prisoners passed by, with tears in their eyes. Even as a child, she understood that those men deeply loved and missed their children, who were now living in harm's way.

Following the war, some of these farm families corresponded with the former prisoners until their deaths. A treasure trove of about 350 letters and photos from German former prisoners has recently been discovered in a home in Tennessee. They are now housed at the Lipscomb University in Nashville. They met by working on that farm, then kept in touch over the years. However, it was secret. The letters were found in a cereal box in a closet and even the children of this woman did not know about them.

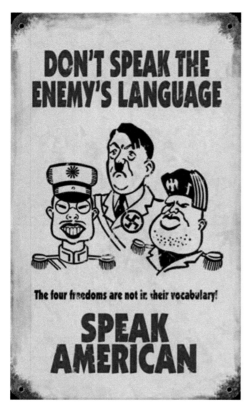

From *"una Storia Segreta"* by Lawrence Distasi. The licensing metadata from the picture claims that it is a "work prepared by an officer or employee of the United States Government as part of that person's official duties."

Entrance to the Vatican Secret Archives. (*Photo by author*)

German prisoners of war at Fort Douglas (UT) in 1917 (crews of German ships). (*Courtesy of Utah Historical Society*)

For many years into the 1970s and 1980s, and as late as 2009, there were reunions and family trips made by former prisoners to their old camps and the farms where they worked. They also visited the graves of their comrades who did not survive to go home at the end of the war.

Of the half-million German immigrants arriving in the United states from 1947–1960, several thousand had spent time here as prisoners of war. The same can be said of Italian immigrants after World War II. They had friends and good experiences here that motivated them to move here themselves.

Even among those enemy aliens who were forced to repatriate at the end of World War II in exchange for Americans and for other reasons, the vast majority had agreed to the arrangement because it guaranteed them the ability to return to the U.S. at a later date. They later used that agreement to return home to the United States. That included Germans, Italians, and Japanese.

Prisoners were moved between Service Command Areas in 1943 as the U.S. built more camps and received more prisoners from overseas. Later, the prisoners were moved within a Service Command as necessary to provide seasonal labor on farms and in canneries as well as other work necessary for civilians as well as the military population.

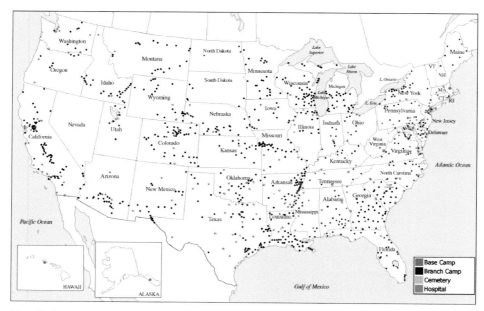

Map of POW camps and hospitals across America. (*Courtesy of John Saffell*)

Using a variety of sources in the United States and Italy, the complete story will be told. Sources cited include military records now housed at the National Archives II (in College Park, MD), documents from the Italian Army Archives in Rome (*Stato Maggiore Esercito*) and *L'Ufficio Informazione Vaticano per I prigionieri di guerra istituito da Pio XII* in the Vatican Secret Archives, as well as many books, articles, websites, and photographs.

Also utilized are interviews with former POWs, guards, translators (and their families), and many other sources both published and unpublished. Their experiences will also be compared to those of German POWs and internees held in America during World War I.

Background

By the time we entered World War II (WWII), almost the whole world was at war. This situation included large numbers of POWs which could no longer be supported by the limited resources of the British and French who captured many of them, primarily in North Africa in 1939.

The U.S. had already prepared plans for camps to house large numbers of enemy aliens, so assisting with prisoners captured by the British was easily incorporated into those general plans. It was determined early that the U.S. would not be imprisoning as many enemy aliens as first planned. The number of resident aliens who matched the original enemy alien profile was much larger than anticipated, so implementing that original plan was not possible.

During World War I (WWI), only 1,346 POWs were held on United States soil. They were the crews of German military ships lying in U.S. ports when the war began. They were held in the same three locations as civilian enemy aliens, plus six additional branch locations for a total of 5,887 prisoners of war. All other prisoners of that war captured by the U.S. were held in France.

Those U.S. locations included the following:

War Prison Barracks #1—Fort McPherson, East Point, GA—100 prisoners maximum.
War Prison Barracks #2—Fort Oglethorpe, Catloosa County, GA—800 prisoners maximum.
War Prison Barracks #3—Fort Douglas, Salt Lake City, UT—406 POWs and 786 enemy aliens.

On March 21, 1918, the POWs were transferred from Fort Douglas to Fort McPherson. On July 19, 1919, 108 conscientious objectors arrived at Fort Douglas from Fort Leavenworth, KS. They were housed in the compound left vacant by the POWs.

Branch camps under the camps in GA:

Camp Devens, Ayer, MA—100 prisoners maximum
Camp Grant, Rockford, IL—100 prisoners maximum
Camp Jackson, Columbia, SC—100 prisoners maximum
Camp Sevier, Greenville, SC—100 prisoners maximum

Monument to German POWs from WWI at Fort Douglas. The U.S. did not separate the enemy aliens from the POWs, so only two of the twenty-one men on this list were POWs. (*Photo by author*)

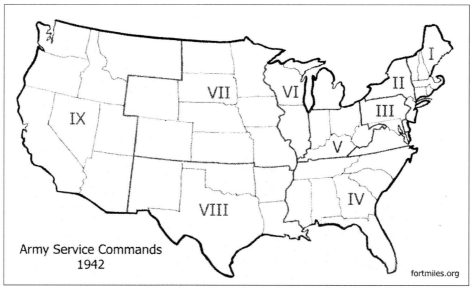

U.S. Service Command areas map. (*National Archives and Records Administration II in College Park, MD, Record Group 389*)

Camp Sherman, near Chillicothe, OH—100 prisoners maximum

   Camp Wadsworth, Spartanburg, SC—100 prisoners maximum

These camps were run by the Provost Marshal General's Office (PMGO) of the U.S. Army. Initially, there were no distinctions between captured German sailors and enemy aliens rounded up from across the U.S. However, it soon became apparent that the two groups were quite different and efforts were made to put different groups into different camps.

   Another camp, called an Internment Camp, was established at Hot Springs, NC and run by the Immigration and Naturalization Service (INS). It held 2,200 Germans from commercial ships in U.S. ports when war broke out in 1914. They were placed at Hot Springs in May 1917 for the remainder of the war. Burials from this location were removed to Chattanooga National Cemetery after that war.

Preparing for War

The military headquarters/training for the 9th Service command moved inland from The Presidio of San Francisco, CA to Fort Douglas, UT at the end of 1941 to make it less vulnerable to a Japanese attack.

The U.S. needed:

1. Labor, since most able-bodied young men were expected in military service and efforts to recruit women into the workforce had only limited success. However, "Rosie the Riveter" became iconic and female pilots as well as clerks (military and civilian), nurses, teachers, and many other occupations gained workers from this effort. Those numbers decreased immediately after the war when the men returned home, but steadily increased as time passed.
2. Supplies for military troops overseas as well as military troops and civilians at home included timber, cotton, tobacco, food (planting, harvesting, canning, fishing), clothing, arms and ammunition and transportation vehicles for land, sea and air.
3. Building and maintenance of new and expanded military installations as well as roads, railways, airfields, dams, and camps for POWs and enemy aliens.

Train at Utah ASF Depot. (*Courtesy of Special Collections Department, Stewart Library, Weber State University*)

Global Situation

POWs held by the British and French were straining their limited supplies so they needed to be farmed out to other Allied nations (Algeria, Australia, Canada, Egypt, Great Britain, India, Kenya, Libya, the Middle East, South Africa, and the U.S.).

POWs were being held in the various theaters of war, but the numbers were much greater than could be used for supply and support behind combat lines. Great Britain held 23,000 German and 250,000 Italian prisoners in August 1942. Plans were made to transport them to places where their care would not remove men from combat and where their labor could be used to ease shortages caused by men away from home.

Generally, ships carrying supplies and men into the European and Mediterranean theaters of war were used to transport POWs back to America, Canada, Australia, etc. While many POWs worried about getting bombed or torpedoed by their own nations, there were few incidents. The SS *Benjamin Contee* was torpedoed off the coast of Algeria on August 16, 1943, by German aircraft. The ship proceeded to Bone, to Algiers, and then to Gibraltar, where emergency repairs were made, then to New York City, arriving January 29, 1944. The bodies of thirty-six unidentifiable Italian prisoners (900 British-held Italian prisoners had been on this ship before the attack) were removed from the most damaged part of the vessel and buried at Long Island National Cemetery.

The German POW population in the U.S. in May 1942 was only thirty-one with one Japanese POW. There were no Italian POWs here at that time.

The Italian POWs were captured by British, French, and American troops between 1939 and 1943 in North Africa and Europe. They first arrived in the U.S. in early 1943 through the New York Port of Embarkation.

For the captured officers and naval crews, interrogation centers were their first stops in America. Fort Hunt, VA, was the first of these centers. These interrogators denied torture and criticized the Bush administration when they were honored near Alexandria as part of the U.S. Army's Freedom Team salute program in 2007. The National Park Service (NPS), particularly the George Washington Memorial Parkway (which now contains the former Fort Hunt), is interviewing veterans of P.O. Box 1142 (as it was known then) to tell their story. The former interrogators include John Gunther Dean, later a career Foreign Service officer and ambassador to Denmark who said "We did it with a certain amount of respect and justice." George Frenkel said, "During the many interrogations, I never laid hands

Vincenzo Lo Giudice is shown here with his Italian Army friends in North Africa. (*Courtesy of his daughter, Carmelina*)

Byron Hot Springs (CA) back door, the entrance for the POWs, Joint U.S. Army and Navy interrogation center. (*Courtesy of Carol A. Jensen, historian at Byron Hot Springs*)

on anyone." He said, "We extracted information in a battle of the wits, I'm proud to say I never compromised my humanity."

The second interrogation center was Byron Hot Springs, CA, also known as P.O. Box 651. Following the example of the British to gain maximum cooperation with excellent living conditions, this former resort spa was used primarily for the highest-ranking German officers and Japanese naval crews while Fort Hunt was used primarily for German naval crews. Information gained at Fort Hunt and Byron Hot Springs was also used later in the murder trials of naval POWs accused of murder in the camps.

The third interrogation center appearing on the camp lists as "restricted listing", the same designation as the two locations above, has recently been exposed as Pine Grove Furnace, NY.

These interrogation centers were run by a combination of Military Intelligence, an agency of the Adjutant General's Office (G-2), and the Office of Naval Intelligence (ONI). Since this was against Geneva Convention rules, they were listed on PMGO lists of POW camps as "restricted listing" camps to conceal their locations.

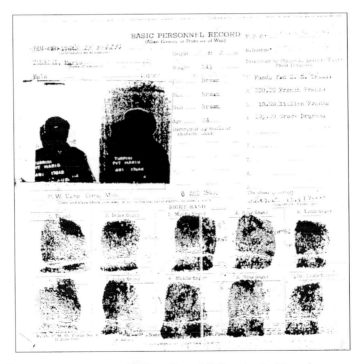

This ID card for Mario Turrini was created at Camp Como, MS. Note that the ID number was crossed out when they realized he already had a POW number assigned by the British who had originally captured him. In the far-right column, you can see that he had coins from France (from his service in Tunisia), Italy (from his Italian Army pay), and Greece (his last duty station before Tunisia). (*Courtesy of his son, Marcello, who lives in Italy*)

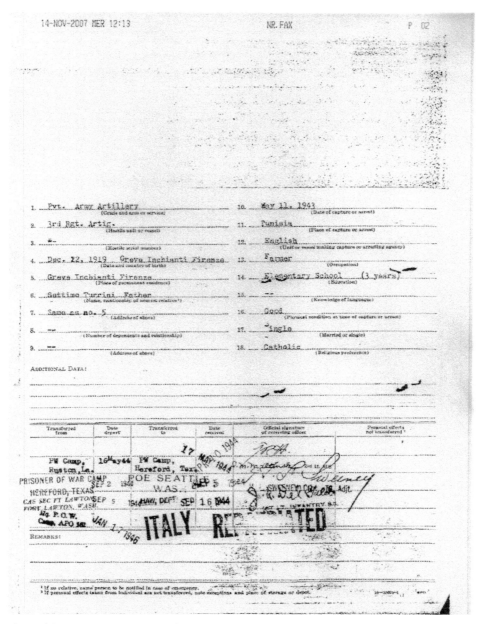

This card for Mario Turrini was created at Camp Ruston, LA, his location after processing at Camp Como. It shows that in May 1944, he was transferred to Camp Hereford, TX. This is part of the sorting process and he was categorized as not cooperative since he did not sign up to be a co-belligerent in the Italian Service Units (ISU) after the fall of Mussolini. In September 1944, he was transferred to the Seattle Port of Entry, particularly Fort Lawton, from which he sailed two weeks later for duty at POW Camp APO 950 (a.k.a. Fort Armstrong), Honolulu, HI. The Italian prisoners were not sure where they were going and there were rumors that they would be sent into combat zones in the Pacific theater.

Planning and Building the Camps

Initially, enemy alien camps were planned for 100,000 internees. However, after it was determined that original parameters for designating enemy aliens as potential threats were too broad and could not be implemented because of the vast numbers of people involved, the camps under construction were repurposed as POW camps. They expected to fill them with POWs already captured by the British, about 100,000.

Lessons learned in WWI led to the separation of POWs (under the PMGO of the Army) and enemy aliens (under the INS within the Department of Justice (DOJ)). Also in the wake of WWI were the agreements made at the Geneva Convention in 1929. It was determined that the U.S. would (usually) follow such agreements not only because of the legal obligations, but also in hopes of reciprocal good treatment by our enemies.

Among those soldiers captured in German uniform were men who considered themselves another nationality, such as Austrian, Czech, Swiss, Italian, Russian, Mongol, Hungarian, Romanian, and more. Among those captured in Japanese uniform were Koreans. Among those captured in Italian uniforms were Slavs (present day Croatia, Bosnia, and Slovenia), Albanians, and Ethiopians. It was quickly learned that these groups needed to be separated in the POW camps both at home and abroad. In many of these groups were men who claimed U.S. citizenship. Their trials were postponed repeatedly until the end of the war when they were sent back to the nation in whose army they had been captured.

Only one of the POW camps had previously been used as WWI POW camp, Fort Douglas, UT. Some were already military installations, like Fort Jay, NY. Some were former Civilian Conservation Corps (CCC) camps, like Fort Hunt, VA. Many were new purchases, like Camp Monticello, AR.

There were several potential standard camp plans, adapted to different climates and geographical considerations, but ultimately, each camp was unique in its layout due to geography and transportation infrastructure. In addition to building barracks, mess halls, warehouses, administrative buildings, and a hospital, the first commanding officer of the Utah ASF Depot POW camp, UT, designated 50 acres nearby to grow crops to help feed the POWs. The crop yield was so bountiful it was shared with the Depot cafeteria, the Depot quartermaster, Bushnell General Hospital (in Brigham City), and the Ogden Air Service Command at nearby Hill Field. A similar assortment of buildings and garden areas was described at most other base camp locations.

Garden at Utah ASF Depot. (*Courtesy of Special Collections Department, Stewart Library, Weber State University*)

Italian prisoners of war in freight yard at Utah ASF Depot. (*Courtesy of Special Collections Department, Stewart Library, Weber State University*)

Managing the Camps

Security was a primary concern. Guards were a combination of military (often older men and wounded combat veterans) and civilian. Sometimes, long-lasting friendships developed between the guards and the POWs they watched, particularly among the interpreters.

In a successful effort to conserve manpower, it was the experience at Utah ASF Depot, UT, that one woman with a dog could patrol the same area as two men.

The POW work details were supervised by guards armed with carbines and rifles. Originally, the ratio was one guard to ten POWs, but over time diminished to one guard to thirty-two prisoners. When U.S. Army personnel was not available, the base commander could supply guards from other sources. Handcuffing or abuse was forbidden. Each of the guard towers in the compound was occupied by a guard equipped with machine guns.

Sometimes, the U.S. Army translators were also guards, like Thomas M. Todaro, who worked at Camp Monticello and later at Fort Leonard Wood, MO. Translators (usually U.S. military) were assigned to camps. However, U.S. military translators for Italian Service Units (ISU) were assigned to the units which moved from camp to camp as needed to provide services.

The POWs were soon discovered to be an uneasy (sometimes dangerous), mix of several nationalities, languages, and ideologies; regardless of their uniform. They were then segregated by nationality and politics and rank. In many camps, the officers were simply held in a separate compound from the enlisted, as directed by the Geneva Convention. However, compounds at Camps Beale, Blanding, McCain and Papago Park were designated for German Naval crews. Camp Alva was for Nazis. Camps Blanding, Campbell, and Devens were anti-Nazi camps. Camps Hereford, Monticello, and Weingarten were for Italian fascists. These divisions into Nazi and anti-Nazi were based on judgments made by G-2, the Army Intelligence unit.

The generalities do not take into account transfers from camp to camp that were frequent and based on additional factors, such as work, health, and relationships. Most POWs did not accurately fall into the above categories; they were young men who grew up in societies with mandatory youth groups and mandatory military service whose families were living in Nazi-controlled locations.

After initial interrogation, the German generals were placed at Camps Clinton and Dermott while Italian generals and officers were at Camp Monticello. Additional German officers were held at Crossville.

POW farm labor with guards. (*Courtesy of Gary Reeves collection of POW artifacts*)

ARMY SERVICE FORCES
NINTH SERVICE COMMAND
POST STOCKADE & PRISON OFFICE
CAMP ADAIR, OREGON

10 May 1944

SPECIAL ORDERS FOR PRISONER CHASERS

1. I will keep this order in my possession at all times while on duty as a prisoner chaser.

2. I will learn the names of prisoners assigned to me for work; and the exact location and kind of work to be done and will see that the prisoners wear their full fatigue uniforms at work.

3. I will not allow my prisoners to separate or get more than fifteen (15) paces from me, or closer than six (6) paces to me. I will keep my prisoners in sight at all times.

4. When I cannot safely guard my prisoners I will return them to the Post Stockade and report the circumstances.

5. I will not allow my prisoners to enter any building, except designated latrines, while at work.

6. I will not smoke, converse with anyone, lean against any object, sit down, discard, or lay aside my arms.

7. I will keep my prisoners constantly at work, giving them one (1) break in the morning and one (1) break in the afternoon.

8. I will immediately return my prisoners to the Post Stockade when "recall from fatigue" is sounded, or when work assigned is finished.

9. If I am ordered to escort my prisoners on a vehicle, I will post myself on one side of the vehicle with prisoners on opposite side. I will maintain a position whereby prisoners are within sight at all times, both on and off of vehicles.

10. If a prisoner attempts to escape, the sentinel or any member of the Main Guard or Prisoner Guard who sees him will call "HALT"; If the prisoner fails to halt when the sentinel has repeated his call, and if there is no possible means of preventing his escape, the sentinel will fire at him. (Par. 44.F / TR 135-15).

11. I will at no time allow my prisoner to congregate or mill around with other prisoners, civilians, or other soldiers.

12. I understand that I am fully responsible for the conduct, and work performed by prisoners assigned to me to guard, and that I am subject to Disciplinary action if I fail to enforce these orders properly or promptly, and report any misconduct on the part of the prisoners to the Post Prison Officer. Phone 2847.

ELLIOTT L. BOURDS
1st Lt., QMC
Police & Prison Officer

Instructions for POW guards, issued at Camp Adair (OR). (*Courtesy of Gary Reeves collection of POW artifacts*)

Above left: This British issue dog tag for an Italian-enlisted POW was on display at the March Air Field Museum display on Camp Haan (CA). (*Photo by author*)

Above right: Thomas M. Todaro, guard and translator. (*Courtesy of his son, Robert*)

Board at Fort Devens (MA) showing those POWs who could work without a guard. (*Courtesy of Gary Reeves collection of POW artifacts*)

Orazio and Angelo Vecchio, brothers and Italian prisoners at Utah ASF Depot. (*Courtesy of Orazio's grandson, Orazio Vecchio, living in Italy*)

I am in an American internment camp.
Sono in un campo d'internamento Americano.

My physical condition is
Il mio stato di salute è OTTIMO

My address is   Ogden Internment Camp
Il mio indirizzo è   Box 20, General Post Office
                        New York, New York, USA

Name
Nome VECCHIO - ORAZIO

Internment Serial No.
No. d'internamento   T 75052

U. S. A. P. O. No.
Officio portale Esercito degli Stati Uniti-No.

Date
Data APR 1 2 1943

GPO   16—27544-1

Standard POW form, filled out for Orazio Vecchio. (*Courtesy of his grandson, Orazio Vecchio*)

G-2 interviewed these officers, however the highest-ranking officer in these interrogation teams was a Major, so not perceived by the POWs as qualified to deal with an officer of higher rank. Consequently, cursory and sometimes erroneous conclusions were drawn, heavily influenced by other high-ranking enemy officers who were invited to participate.

A glaring example is the input of Italian General Trezzani who used the opportunity to cast doubt (and worse, calling another Italian general a Nazi). He used this ploy on officers of similar rank to promote himself with the Americans. He used it to great advantage to become the head of the Italian Service Units (ISU) in the U.S. and later in charge of rebuilding the Italian Army in post-war Italy.

Additionally, Italian Royalists and career army were considered fascist while German career army were considered Nazi, simply for participating in youth groups (required) or in support of Franco (military service) in Spain. There was so much more to the story.

Public opinion was most loudly expressed by those with the greatest fear of enemy camps in their towns, or by those who hoped to profit from the use of POW labor in their businesses. Most Americans viewed the new camps with caution, but acceptance, and gradually came to appreciate the additional civilian jobs and affordable labor source. Some even developed friendships which lasted long after the war ended.

Each prisoner was processed either when captured or when they arrived in the U.S. This process included searching, delousing, disinfecting, fumigation, bathing, registration, clothing issue, quartering, and medical inspection.

Giovanni D'Onofrio (third from left) and POW friends at Utah ASF Depot. (*Courtesy of his children, Vincent, Orazio, and Janice*)

Carlo Selmi and POW friends at Utah ASF Depot. (*Courtesy of his son, Andrea, living in Italy*)

Life in the Camps

The maximum number of German POWs held in the continental U.S. was 371,683 in May 1945. Italian POWs (continental U.S.) reached a maximum of 51,156 in November 1944. Japanese POWs (continental U.S.) reached a maximum of 5,413 in August 1945. There were POW camps in every state except Vermont, plus the territories of Hawaii and Alaska.

The POWs were placed into companies of 250 men each, eight companies to a compound (2,000 men), with two compounds at Ogden ASF Depot in 1943. Later, one compound at Ogden ASF Depot was composed of Italian Service Units while the other housed German POWs who were willing to work there. They were the first camp to work the two groups together, with Germans supervising Italians and the opposite.

Each base camp had a station hospital, staffed by both Americans and POWs. Utah ASF Depot station hospital had 100 beds, like most station hospitals. Since many POWs arrived in poor health due to long imprisonment and poor diet (both before and after imprisonment), that hospital admitted over 2,000 men by June 1944 after opening only eighteen months earlier.

Housing and furnishings at first met, and then exceeded the Geneva Convention requirements. Since the camps were in different locations, some utilized barracks and some hutments (smaller housing units) while the temporary and seasonal camps often used tents. The Geneva Convention required mattresses only for officers. Eventually, most permanent camps had mattresses, pillows, and pillow cases on iron and wooden beds for enlisted men as well as officers.

General hospitals, run by the Surgeon General of Army Service Forces (ASF), were in each region, utilizing a POW wing to facilitate security. In 1944, they became more specialized to receive all patients from theaters of operations, plus patients needing specialized treatment in the zone of interior.

Those station hospitals with airfields were overseen by the Air Surgeon of the Army Air Force (AAF). In 1944, regional hospitals (a new designation), station hospitals, and convalescent centers were now run by both the ASF and AAF. The regional hospitals were to serve as general hospitals for zone of interior patients. These designations are rarely mentioned in the population lists in the National Archives.

The station hospitals were generally staffed with an American officer of the Medical Corps and three POW attendants with medical training. The surgical staff included an

American Medical officer, a nurse, an enlisted man, and three POW attendants with medical training. POWs also served as lab technicians. The hospital mess was under the mess officer with a civilian nurse and a mess sergeant. It was staffed by two U.S. Army mess sergeants, one POW mess sergeant, and four POW cooks. Provisions were made for special diets.

Mental patients in Utah were sent to Bushnell General Hospital, UT, while extreme cases were sent to Mason General Hospital, NY. Dental care was also provided at the station hospitals for the POWs treating abscesses, and doing extractions, fillings, and gum treatments. At Utah ASF Depot, over 17,000 dental cases were treated during the year of 1943–1944.

Upon arrival, the POWs were issued clothing and blankets that were maintained and replaced as needed. The Red Cross in New York was issuing two pairs of blankets per man and a uniform that might be the dark blue with white PW lettering, or an old U.S. Army uniform, plus the uniform he arrived wearing. Not many had overcoats; some came with English overcoats, black with a black diamond on the back.

The POWs were supposed to be adequately, comfortably, and properly clothed in accordance with the climate conditions in which they lived and worked according to the Geneva Convention of 1929. The War Department later determined that dark blue was

Utah ASF Depot hospital grounds. (*Courtesy of Special Collections Department, Stewart Library, Weber State University*)

Utah ASF Depot hospital steps. (*Courtesy of Special Collections Department, Stewart Library, Weber State University*)

a preferable uniform color since it would not be mistaken for the American khaki. They were also provided with woolen underwear, cotton underwear, woolen socks and cotton socks, woolen shirts and cotton shirts, two pairs of trousers in either wool or denim, two cotton coats in wool or khaki, a wool overcoat, a raincoat, woolen caps and hats, cotton hats and caps, shoes and overshoes, gloves, and two heavy woolen blankets. When an item wore out, it was immediately replaced. The clothing was class X or class B, American issue.

Some camps had laundry facilities with machines while some had wash rooms where laundry was done by hand.

Education included classes in English, history, and democracy plus clerical and equipment training. Supplies were provided for many art projects and newsletter production.

Newspapers were produced by the prisoners at most of the larger camps. There is a collection of Italian POW newsletters at Utah State University. There is a large collection of German POW newsletters at the Library of Congress. Many of these newsletters can be found at local colleges and historical societies.

Their food was the equivalent of that issued to American servicemen (type A field ration), according to the Geneva Convention, although substitutions were made to recognize ethnic preferences. The Italian POWs had an increase in rice, spaghetti, macaroni, noodles, and pasta with decreases in meats and baked beans. Germans had an increase in potatoes and a decrease in beans. Meals were served three times daily. Special menus were prepared on Thanksgiving, Christmas, New Year's, and other holidays. For many prisoners, these rations exceeded their military experience. The average prisoner at Utah ASF Depot gained 15 pounds.

Utah ASF Depot POW class with civilian instructor and U.S. Army guard. (*Courtesy of Special Collections Department, Stewart Library, Weber State University*)

POW newspaper from Fort McClellan, AL. (*Courtesy of Gary Reeves collection of POW artifacts*)

Some beautiful art was created in the camps; this piece from Colorado shows a sense of humor as well. (*Courtesy of Gary Reeves collection of POW artifacts*)

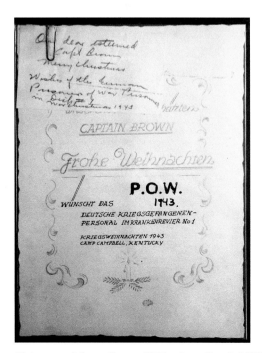

Christmas card from a German POW at Camp Campbell (KY). (*Courtesy of Gary Reeves collection of POW artifacts*)

The POWs were their own cooks and bakers, being paid the same wage as those working in all occupations both in and outside of the camps. However, each camp commander had some autonomy and after the liberation of concentration camps in Germany, some camps restricted food allowances for POWs well below Geneva Convention (Hereford, TX, is infamous for its dietary cuts in 1945).

Many services were available for POWs, some in accord with the Geneva Convention and some additional benefits. They included canteens and camp stores where a POW could spend the pay (in coupons) he earned working on such items as beer, cigarettes, and gold jewelry (high-quality necklaces, wedding rings, and rosaries were in high demand by the Italian POWs at Utah ASF Depot). The profits from the sales were returned to the POWs in the form of free beer, cigarettes, and theater tickets.

Some POW photos show the decorations (pin-ups) in their personal areas. These could include small pictures of national leaders and flags and emblems, but large displays were limited to funerals and religious services.

Recreation supplies were provided for many sports, although soccer was most popular. Other equipment included baseball, softball, basketball, football, boxing, volleyball, croquet, horse shoes, badminton, and table tennis. Many game sets were also provided for the POWs including dominoes, Chinese checkers, checkers, backgammon, India, bingo,

Italian POW cooks at Utah ASF Depot. (*Courtesy of Special Collections Department, Stewart Library, Weber State University*)

Utah ASF Depot, Italian POW bakery. (*Courtesy of Special Collections Department, Stewart Library, Weber State University*)

chess, playing cards, etc. The POW often constructed their own volleyball courts, baseball diamonds, and soccer fields.

POW contacts with families and others included inspection visits from the Red Cross, YMCA, Swiss government, and other welfare organizations. Each POW was permitted two letters and one post card per week, written in ink (not pencil). Also, when necessary, one business letter per week was allowed. Special stationary was provided, so it was limited to the lines on the forms. Free mailing was applied to all letters, postcards, and parcels less than four pounds, addressed to or sent by a POW through the U.S. Postal Service. Each POW was also allowed, at his own expense, one prepaid cable or telegram per month. In the event of a serious emergency (death or serious illness), and at the discretion of the base commander, more than one per month may be sent.

Incoming mail for Italian POWs from relatives in the U.S. was enormous. In two or three months alone, 300–500 packages were received at Utah ASF Depot. The POWs sent many gifts to their relatives in this country and to those outside the continental U.S. Correspondence to POWs was permitted from anyone. However, POWs could only write to and receive packages from family members such as wives, grandparents, parents, siblings, aunts, uncles, children, nieces, and nephews.

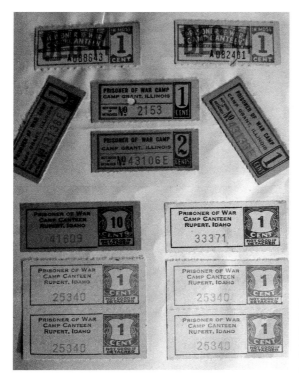

Ration coupons were issued by each camp, but the format was standardized as shown here of coupons from Camp Livingston (LA), Camp Grant (IL), and Camp Rupert (ID). (*Courtesy of Gary Reeves collection of POW artifacts*)

This photo was taken for a news service of the canteen at Camp Custer (MI). (*Courtesy of Gary Reeves collection of POW artifacts*)

Matchbooks were made for Fort Robinson (NE) and many other camps. (*Courtesy of Gary Reeves collection of POW artifacts*)

Some camps issued cards for special items, like this beer card. (*Courtesy of Gary Reeves collection of POW artifacts*)

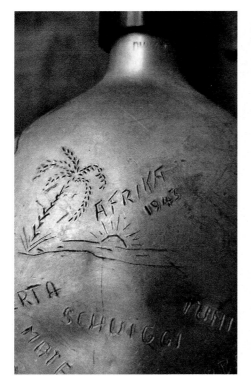

Of course, people create art out of whatever is available, as evidenced by this water canteen with inscriptions from this German soldier's time in Africa in 1943. (*Courtesy of Gary Reeves collection of POW artifacts*)

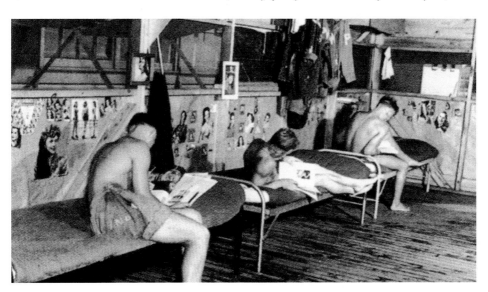

Barracks at Camp Atterbury (IN). (*Courtesy of Alessandro de Gaetano*)

Theatrical productions at Fort Lewis. (*Courtesy of Gary Reeves collection of POW artifacts*)

The Edgewood Arsenal POW Camp in Maryland had soccer teams and here's one photocard dated 1944. Had to keep there German POWs busy! They look like a group of High School students. ADDED 2ed ONE!

POW soccer team at Edgewood Arsenal (MD). (*Courtesy of Gary Reeves collection of POW artifacts*)

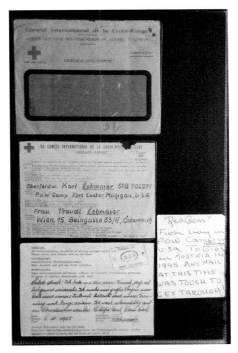

Above left: This letter was sent from a British POW camp in Garian (Libya) to a POW in Camp Wheeler, GA. (*Courtesy of Gary Reeves collection of POW artifacts*)

Above right: This letter was sent through the Red Cross from a POW Camp in Custer (MI) to a young woman in Austria. Some letters were also sent through the Vatican as an alternative to the U.S. mail. (*Courtesy of Gary Reeves collection of POW artifacts*)

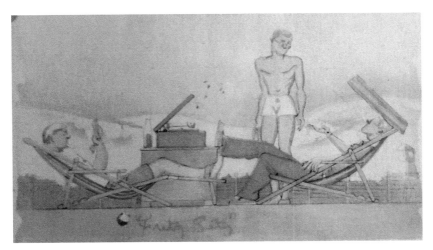

This postcard was designed by a German POW and printed by the YMCA. (*Courtesy of Gary Reeves collection of POW artifacts*)

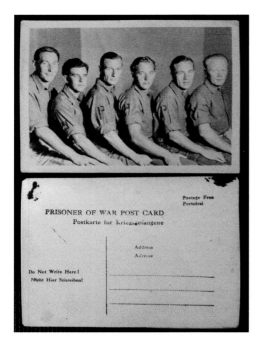

Postcard with a group photo of German POWs. (*Courtesy of Gary Reeves collection of POW artifacts*)

Many camps and military installations had their own postcards. (*Courtesy of Robert Todaro from his father's duty assignment there as a POW translator and guard*)

Postcards with a group photo of German POWs from Camp Swift (TX). (*Courtesy of Gary Reeves collection of POW artifacts*)

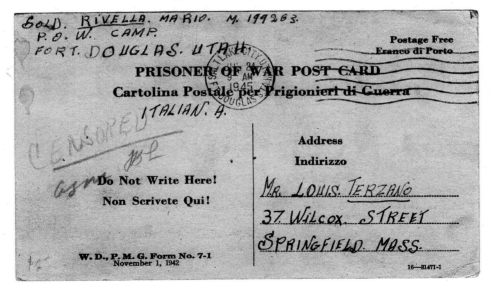

POW postcard front from Fort Douglas (UT). (*Courtesy of Dennis H. Pack*)

POW postcard back from Fort Douglas (UT). (*Courtesy of Dennis H. Pack*)

Acrobats on stage at Fort Lewis (WA). (*Courtesy of Gary Reeves collection of POW artifacts*)

ISU band at Utah USF Depot. (*Courtesy of Andrea Selmi, son of Carlo Selmi, clarinet player in this band (third from left), living in Italy*)

Most camps had bands and/or orchestras made up of their POW population. At many locations, concerts were held once a week. The orchestras also played for stage shows and gave monthly concerts. Many instruments were provided by the Catholic church; others were loaned by the Depot Quartermaster. At some camps, the local schools and communities provided instruments.

The ISU band at Utah ASF Depot played for dances each week, both at the POW camp and at St. Joseph's Catholic Church in Ogden. The dances were a good place to meet the local girls. The POWs were taken to the church by bus from the camp. Separate dances (different nights) for officers and enlisted POWs to adhere to Geneva Convention.

Religion was also a part of camp life. At first, religious services at Ogden, UT, were held in the open with an improvised pulpit. Later, a recreation hall was used part time for morning Mass. An empty barrack was utilized as a regular chapel for weekdays. Later, the old Compound One Headquarters building became the Main Chapel and accommodated about 300 POWs for daily Mass. When Compound Two was activated, one of its recreational halls was provided for chapel functions and accommodated about 700. This camp was Italian, so only Catholic services were required. The hospital also held Mass on Sunday. When the camp opened a German compound, a Lutheran minister provided services on Sunday in addition to the Catholic services for the German POWs. Every U.S. camp had a similar regard for religious services.

While POWs were not allowed to donate blood (prohibited by the PMGO and Geneva Convention), they were allowed to make voluntary contributions to specific organizations, such as the Red Cross and the YMCA. A minor political group at Utah ASF Depot, the Republicans, collected $80 for war bonds and offered to donate blood; they offered the money to the Infantile Paralysis Fund because they believed it was a good cause.

Escapes were expected and did occur at several locations. Most of them were short in duration and distance, usually ending with an easy capture or surrender since the object was just to get outside the fence for a while. Some were more serious, with bigger plans and groups of men, also usually ending in surrender. Just a few men were able to remain at large until many years after the war ended. No reports of sabotage or terrorism were ever associated with these escapes.

The most interesting was eleven attempted escapes in the first week of May 1945 at Boswell Ranch in Corcoran, CA. They totaled twenty prisoners, one of whom made three attempts in this time. The most successful attempt was on January 3 when three men scaled the fence amid bullets from the guards. A fourth escaped a few hours later. All four men turned themselves in at the La Hacienda Ranch, 20 miles away, only three days later. The foreman there called the sheriff to collect the POWs.

There were pets among the POWs, sometimes traveling with them from camp to camp.

POW work included occupations required for the maintenance of the camps, such as cooking, cleaning, clothing and shoe repairs, landscaping, etc.

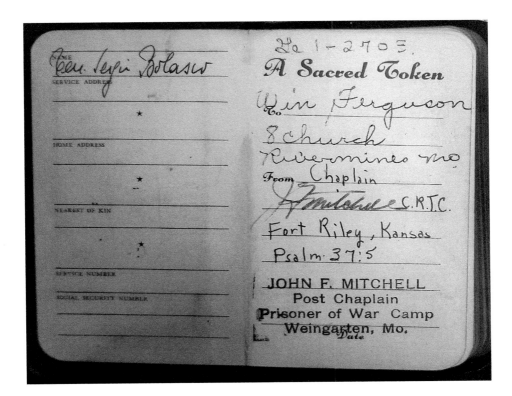

Above: This Bible seems to have gone from Win Ferguson to Italian Lt. Sergei Bolasco after being presented by a U.S. Army chaplain who served at both Fort Riley (KS) and POW Camp Weingarten (MO). (*Courtesy of Gary Reeves collection of POW artifacts*)

Left: Madonna made and placed at Camp Lockett (CA) near their housing area by Italian POWs. (*Courtesy of Mountain Empire Historical Society*)

A group of Italian POWs at Camp Lockett, CA pose with their priest and their dog. (*Courtesy of Mountain Empire Historical Society*)

In 1953, *Collier's* magazine published a story about five German POW still missing. One escaped from near Bastrop (LA), one from Las Cruces (NM), one from Fort Dix (NJ), one from Deming (NM), and one from Camp Butner (NC). (*Courtesy of Gary Reeves collection of POW artifacts*)

They also were hired out for canning and farming in the community, including pruning orchards and planting as well as harvesting. They also worked on dams, railroads, orchards, mining, quarrying, and forestry. The businesses and farmers paid the government a minimum wage and the POWs were paid 80 cents a day, comparable to the wage for a civilian day laborer.

Even the Ogden Chamber of Commerce hired POWs, and Italian POWs at Fort Monmouth, NJ, were making violins.

Other POWs were working on occupations labeled military, such as at hospitals, supply offices, post exchanges, construction, dying uniforms, landscaping, and woodworking.

Sometimes POWs worked on community service projects outside the camp. The Catholic Church of St. Mary's in Umbarger, TX, was beautifully decorated with murals and other artwork by Italian POWs from nearby Camp Hereford.

The POWs were paid a minimum wage consistent with civilian day laborers if they did work (about $30/month for enlisted) or $24 a month for officers who were not allowed to work. Those men who did work were paid $0.80–1.20 each day depending on if working for local farmers or private companies. This was paid to them in coupons they could use at the Canteen, although ISU members could receive one-third of their pay in cash to use in town. ISU members also received pay that was slightly higher (sometimes $1.50/day) to match the pay of American soldiers. That rate of pay was based on their rank in the ISU, not their Italian Army rank. An office of the Italian Army that made sure all the former POWs received their due pay was opened at the end of the war and continued until very recently. I worked in their offices in 2004 and was able to obtain records of transfers from camp to camp and the health record for a POW (with authorization from his son).

Geneva Convention required that officers be separated from enlisted men. They were sometimes in a compound next to the enlisted men and had otherwise the same types of facilities.

Murals painted by Italian POWs at St. Mary's Catholic Church at Umbarger (TX). (*Courtesy of John Saffell*)

A Papal Delegate visited the Italian POWs at Camp Weingarten (MO). (*Courtesy of Gary Reeves collection of POW artifacts*)

Clearly, this is not the first time the folks in town have seen POWs going past; the boy on a bicycle is not even looking at them and the teenage girls are interested spectators. (*Courtesy of Gary Reeves collection of POW artifacts*)

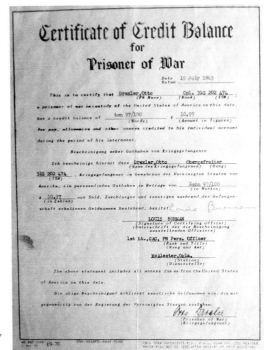

This form from Camp McAlester (OK) shows the accounting made by the U.S. Army when the POWs were processed to return home. (*Courtesy of Gary Reeves collection of POW artifacts*)

Italian Service Units

The fall of Mussolini and resultant change in that government's position in the war from Axis to Allied required some changes regarding Italian POWs. It was quickly determined that releasing them would not be the best solution. The original idea of Italian POWs being organized into units to provide labor similar to the Civilian Conservation Corps (CCC) was first proposed by the U.S. Secretary of War in October 1943. This would require separation of fascist Italian POWs from those willing to work for the war effort as co-belligerents.

[They would be] attached to and placed under the command of the U.S. Army...Therefore, the plan included these features: (1) Italian prisoners would be organized into numbered Italian service companies consisting of 5 officers and 177 enlisted men...(4) An Italian service unit headquarters would be established under ASF and would be commanded by an American officer...The new plan provided for Italian Service Units (ISUs) to be organized from volunteer Italian PW officers, non-commissioned officers, and enlisted men under approved tables of organization and equipment, less weapons. Initially, two U.S. Army officers and 10 enlisted men were to be attached to each unit for supervision; but these were to be reduced, consistent with efficiency and security, to a minimum of one officer and five enlisted men.

The ranking Italian general over the new ISU on January 26, 1944, Claudio Trezzani, states:

The units should be commanded by Italian officers, in this proportion; one first or second lieutenant for 30 to 35 enlisted men (platoon), one captain for 4 platoons (company), one senior officer for 3 companies (battalion), one colonel for 3 battalions (regiment).

That letter is followed in the Italian Army file at Stato Maggiore Esercito in Rome by an apparent American response with no name or date attached:

It is contemplated organizing Italian Service Units according to American tables of organization with Italian military personnel in all authorized positions, American officers and enlisted men in the smallest possible numbers will be attached as custodians, for liaison, to issue operational directives, sign payrolls and charges, and have general responsibility for the units to higher American authority.

Italian Service Units at Utah ASF Depot. (*Courtesy of Special Collections Department, Stewart Library, Weber State University*)

Italian Service Unit English Class at Camp Warren (WY). (*Courtesy of Gary Reeves collection of POW artifacts*)

Italian Generals Frattini and De Simone were moved to ISU headquarters at Fort Wadsworth from Camp Monticello.

The ISU program was under the command of Brig. General J. M. Eager, from the PMGO. The ASF retained the responsibilities of plans, policies and procedures as well as the designation and strength of units and training programs and doctrines. Each unit had American personnel of one officer and five enlisted men at a minimum. Service commands were responsible for all other ISU functions and activities. Interviews with former translators assigned to those units confirmed that one American NCO was a translator for the unit.

The ISU had increased responsibilities resulting in increased privileges for the 65 percent of Italian POWs who signed up to serve in Italian Service Units. The new units were activated progressively with 600 POWs organized in the first week of March 1944, 1,000 for the first two weeks of April, 3,000 the third week in April, and 4,000 each succeeding week until completed. While a letter was sent to the camps from Badoglio in Rome, it was vague and general; also, the Italian king never spoke (wrote) on the subject. This left many men in confusion as to the best course of action. Their families were in German occupied Italy and many feared repercussions for such a visible support of their former enemy. The screening from ISU to POW and reverse was continuous to ensure that only the most cooperative POWs were allowed the privileges of the ISU.

Those men who signed the agreement to join the ISU were given new positions and units and now lived in separate compounds than the POWs who did not sign the agreement.

Those POWs who did not join the ISU were classified as Fascist. Instruction in English stressed in these new units, while the same housing and wages applied, with the addition of 10 cents a day for a gratuitous allowance, sometimes more depending on the work and on their ranks in the new units. Two-thirds of the wage was paid in coupons and one-third in cash. Rules against fraternization between members of ISU and American military did not apply. ISU service clubs were created to give them greater access to reading materials and a quiet place to relax since they did not have access to the U.S. Army clubs. Dances and other special events were organized through the ISU service clubs.

Training programs for ISU were the same as for American personnel on similar jobs, less tactics and weapons training.

Work restrictions imposed by Geneva Convention were lifted with the consent of the Badoglio government of Italy, except for combat, work at ports of embarkation within continental U.S., and work with explosives. Their efforts released U.S. personnel for overseas duties and helped to bring about the successful conclusion of the war.

ISU units began to ship to European theater to assist with support and supply from Africa and into Italy as part of the Liberation of Italy in the following theaters of operation: North Africa, Eastern European, and Mediterranean. Apparently, some of these units were moved overseas at the discretion of the ISU command and the PMGO was not informed.

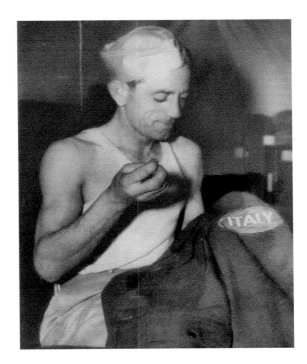

Sewing on his new ISU patch at Fort Wayne (MI). (*Courtesy of Gary Reeves collection of POW artifacts*)

Italian Service Club at Utah ASF Depot. (*Courtesy of Special Collections Department, Stewart Library, Weber State University*)

Official photos were taken of the men in their new uniforms. Note that this photo of Vincenzo Lo Giudice, provided by his daughter, Carmelina, does not yet have patches for rank attached.

Mail restrictions were reduced to the same standards as American personnel for domestic correspondence. Regulations were the same as POWs for international mail. The new ISU uniforms were the same khaki as U.S. uniforms, with a patch (Italy) on the left shoulder. At least one man was court-martialed for removing the Italian patch on a night out on the town, leading to accusations of being AWOL. However, he was simply reprimanded instead of sent to a POW camp.

The POWs and their employers and guards were not supposed to fraternize. Yet, of course, they did. While some of the initial contact was antagonistic, many friendships and romances resulted.

ISU men were permitted weekend passes when signed out by a sponsor. Many Italian communities utilized these privileges to give some of the ISU men a family gathering, social activity, or dance. Some of the dances at the ISU Service Club included invitations to young women in the community.

Additionally, ISU members were given day passes into town for movies, dances, and just sightseeing. In Ogden, buses were used to transport ISU men from their barracks to St. Joseph's Catholic church in downtown Ogden for dances. Of course, the greatest attraction was meeting and dancing with American girls.

Some of these meetings resulted in marriages. The POWs could not marry, but once engaged, and returned (by June 1946), the troop transports bringing GIs home were taking these women with their escorts to Italy with the proper paperwork to marry so they could return to the U.S. with their new husbands. Several of these couples settled in the Inland Empire of Southern California. Six of these men's experiences are described in detail in Susan Ann Meier's Master's thesis.

Some of these meetings had unhappy endings. The local culture was against marrying a man of a different ethnic or religious background, plus some families feared that their girls would follow the men to Italy and never return. So those romances were discouraged, even after they created children. Some of those children were adopted out, while some stayed with their mothers who married other men here in the U.S. after the war. Some of those children have sought their Italian families all their lives. Fortunately, we have assisted with some happy reunions.

Public opinion varied as shown in a variety of newspapers from those years. There were some escapes, usually associated with meeting a girl outside the camp for reasons that had nothing to do with national security.

The Italian POWs held a unique position as both POWs and Allies that created different experiences for them than for their German counterparts. In Oregon and Washington and other ISU locations, these differences meant more opportunities to not only work with the residents, but also to socialize with them. The resulting friendships (and some marriages) show the very positive results of their experiences under very difficult circumstances.

Death in the Camps

A total of 1,075 burials—including 880 Germans (includes three Russians, four Austrians, one Yugoslavian, one Czech and one Turk), 172 Italians, twenty-three Japanese (includes one Korean)—out of 1,076 POWs who died while held in the U.S. during World War II.

Many of the larger camps had their own cemeteries. After the war, the cemeteries from those camps, which had been closed and some other locations, were moved to national cemeteries to provide the perpetual care demanded by the Geneva Convention.

While most of the headstones were standard issue for U.S. military, there are some exceptions. At Fort Douglas, Eilert's stone was put up by the POWs with the permission of the camp commander and paid for by the POWs.

The funeral services were often attended by Americans as well as POWs, sometimes also a POW choir and/or band and a symbolic series of shots were fired by a military guard.

Rumors insist that most of the POWs who died here were shipped home. The truth is that the U.S. Government was willing to ship them, if the family bore the cost. Of course, most of the families were simply unable to bear that burden at the end of a war they lost. Only one Italian, Renato Facchini, was returned to Italy before February 1947, while Francesco Erriquez was returned to Italy in 2011. Apparently, none of the Germans were returned since the names in the original reports match the current cemetery records.

Some of the deaths were accidents in the course of work or recreation. Others were later deemed murders by Nazi extremists. Some were suicides, particularly at the end of the war.

There was unrest among the African-American units at Fort Lawton because they were segregated from the other U.S. soldiers, but the Italian POWs were allowed to shop in the Post Exchange with those from non-African-American units. So when one of the Italian POWs was found strangled by hanging, three African-American soldiers were convicted of murder and another forty convicted of rioting. While none were executed, all received discharges for bad conduct which negatively affected the rest of their lives. They were finally exonerated in 2007, primarily because of the excellent research proving their innocence in *On American Soil* by Jack Hamann in 2005. Hamann also raises a suspicion that Olivotto was murdered by a U.S. Army guard who was court-martialed for not being at his post during the time of the death.

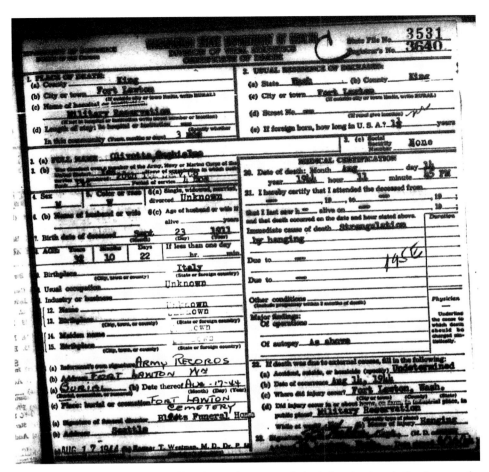

Note that the cause of death for Guglielmo Olivotto shows strangulation by hanging, but whether it was murder or suicide is undetermined. (*Death Certificates from Washington State Archives*)

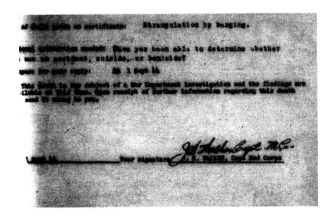

This funeral was held at Camp Monticello, AR. (*Courtesy of Robert Todaro*)

The military honor guard with rifles for a military salute at a funeral at Camp Swift (TX). (*Courtesy of Gary Reeves collection of POW artifacts*)

Death cards were printed by the family back home in Germany and Italy. This one is for a man who died at Glendon (MN), a temporary camp under Camp Algona (IA). Someone thoughtfully attached a photo of his headstone located at Fort Riley (KS). (*Courtesy of Gary Reeves collection of POW artifacts*)

Returning Home (1945–46)

The end of the war was cause for celebration for the POWs who could now look forward to returning home. Their newsletters often contained cartoons expressing these feelings.

Certain camps were designated as separation centers (like Haan, CA) and the POWs were moved through them, then on to ports of embarkation on both coasts for the trip home. The first returned were the Italian officers as co-belligerents. The next group was the ISU members, then the rest.

The Geneva Convention of 1929 required that POWs be returned home at the end of a war. However, the large numbers provided some logistics problems. Generally, troop ships bringing U.S. troops home turned around full of POWs. However, treaties with all countries provided that some of the POWs (not ISU) were returned to France, the USSR and Great Britain to assist with reconstruction efforts. Some of the men in Great Britain and France worked there as long as four years before returning home. The USSR finally released the surviving prisoners ten years later.

Warnings were made regarding German POWs scheduled to be returned to their families and homes in the USSR. It was only after the first group was killed on the dock by the crew of the Soviet vessel which met them that other arrangements were made for those men.

Some POWs claimed status as U.S. citizens and requested permission to stay, but were returned to avoid the legal complications.

Some locations requested that their POWs stay long enough to complete the fall harvest and that was permitted when it could be arranged. The last POWs were repatriated (out of the U.S.) by June 30, 1946, except 141 Germans, twenty Italians, and one Japanese serving sentences in U.S. penal institutions. Two Germans were not repatriated; they revealed themselves many years later, perhaps more since none are shown as missing on PMGO reports.

A large number of ports were utilized as departure points for the returning POWs. They included:

Los Angeles, CA	Hampton Roads, VA	San Francisco, CA
Charleston, SC	New York, NY	Seattle, WA
New Orleans, LA	Boston, MA	Halifax, Nova Scotia.

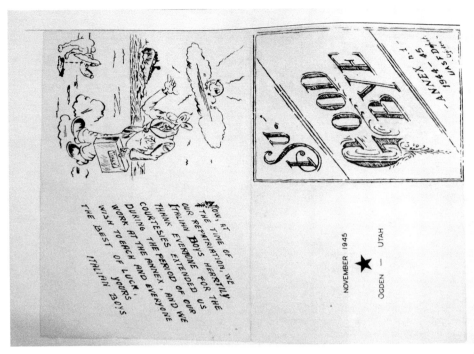

This goodbye note from the Italian boys at Utah ASF Depot was saved by Mario Saggese, one of those boys, and used here courtesy of his daughter, living in the United States.

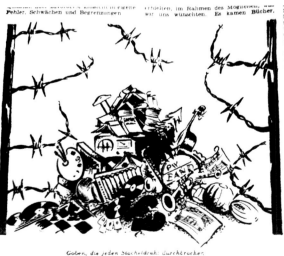

The broken barbed wire and discarded items of entertainment show that while their time as prisoners is ended, so is their leisure time since they now need to rebuild their homes and families. (*Courtesy of Gary Reeves collection of POW artifacts*)

This cartoon showing the camp for sale is much more lighthearted. (*Courtesy of Gary Reeves collection of POW artifacts*)

Those same troop vessels were used to transport American fiancées of POWs to Naples and Genoa. These American war brides often spent a few months in Italy to complete the red tape required for a marriage there and assisting their new families in rebuilding. They then brought their husbands home to America. These stories were shared by Pat and Maria Pisani and by Beth Giordana, war brides and American girls who made the trip to Italy to marry their former POW husbands.

Part of the logistics meant that after the U.S. troops returned home, their European war brides and families were shipped home on the same troop ships, slightly modified to accommodate families with small children. Be sure to see the Cary Grant movie, *I Was a Male War Bride*, which is more funny than factual, but it is based on the real transport of war brides from Europe to America.

Other former POWs made the move to live in the U.S. from ten–twenty years later. They settled in areas where they had worked as POWs, apparently in nearly every location in the country. Only local newspapers have these stories, so it is hard to get statistics. I recently found an article, "Returning to America: German Prisoners of War and the American Experience" by Barbara Schmitter Heisler; the details are in the bibliography.

The trip to marry in Italy was made by a young woman from Louisville, KY, who had met her husband when he was a prisoner at Camp Atterbury, Indiana. They had met at a dance sponsored by the local Italian-American community for the Italian POWs. I met this lovely woman at a POW reunion at Camp Atterbury in 2010 along with her children. They were regular attendees at this annual event and had wonderful stories to share. They also have a display at the Camp Atterbury Museum, across the road from the main gate to Camp Atterbury, now a Reserve Military Training Facility.

This wedding announcement is a portion of the museum display of the Codispoti family, a former Italian POW who settled in the area of Camp Atterbury (IN). (*Photo by author*)

Of course, most of the former POWs returned to their wives and sweethearts in Italy. This is the wedding announcement for Vincenzo Lo Giudice, provided by his daughter, Carmelina.

This book of art was apparently created during his POW years and published later. (*Courtesy of Gary Reeves collection of POW artifacts*)

After the War

Some of the camps were determined to be surplus, so the property was auctioned off and the land was sold or transferred to another Federal or State agency. This was a thorough process, leaving behind very little in the way of buildings to mark the former camps today.

Some of the locations had their designations changed from Camp to Fort, some were originally Forts, but called Camps along with the rest in the PMGO records.

The POW personnel records were returned to other nations in whose military they served in 1955.

The German records are now available at:
Deutsche Dienstelle (WASt)
Postfach 51 06 57
D-13400 Berlin
Germany

The Italian records are now available at:
Ministero della Difesa
via Mattia Battistini, 113, 7 Piano
00167 Roma
Italy

The Japanese records are now available at:
Military History Department National Institute for Defense Studies
2-2-1 Nakameguro, Meguro-ku
Tokyo, 153-8648
Japan

The former POWs held in the U.S. mostly held good memories of their time here. Some returned to become U.S. citizens, like Ernst Bulkat who lived in Orem, UT. Information on them can usually be found in local papers in the 1970s and 1980s, when local news groups interviewed them in a resurgence of interest in the history of the area during WWII.

Some former POWs returned as tourists to show their families where they'd spent part of the war. Some groups held reunions of groups of POWs who had been at a particular location to facilitate their return there with some ceremony and lots of memories.

Some diaries and recollections have been published by former POWs. See Erichsen, Heino R. *The Reluctant Warrior: Former German POW Finds Peace in Texas* for the story of a man who later became a U.S. citizen. The grandson of one of the Italian generals, Maurizio Parri, published his grandfather's war time diaries in *Il Giuramento; Generale a El Alamein, prigioniero in America (1942–1945).*

Some former POWs have been gracious about allowing interviews at reunions, such as Adriano Angerilli, Enzio Luciolli, Giuseppe Margotilli, and Fernando Togni (pictured below). Some of the former, guards, prisoners, and their families have become available for interviews using email, like Ernst Bulkat, Mario Iannantuoni, and August Orsini. On other occasions, I am able to interview the children or grandchildren of a former POW in Italy or the U.S.

In 2009, one of the last reunions of former POWs visited the chapel built by POWs at Camp Hereford, TX. This is indicative of a growing awareness that these memories and relationships must be preserved through reunions, books, lectures, and movies.

Some local magazines and newspapers have done stories on the camps and published interviews with former POWs returning to visit, or who had moved back to the area where they had been imprisoned. Some of these have been preserved by the newspaper, some by local historians, colleges, and historical societies.

A documentary video, *Prisoners in Paradise*, DVD, directed by Camilla Calamandrei tells some of the stories of several former Italian POWs.

Some local TV stations did interviews with surviving former POWs living in their communities in the 1970s and 1980s, like KUED and KSL in Salt Lake City, UT. Some local colleges (Special Collections, Stewart Library, Weber State University) created video archives containing interviews of former POWs and their families and former guards and other employees who had interaction with POWs.

Some former POWs, guards, and their families donated their diaries and photos to local historical societies, like Drew County Historical Museum in Monticello, Arkansas. Some donated to the National Archives (NARA) in College Park, Maryland. Some donated to the Stato Maggiore Esercito in Rome, Italy. I expect more will be found in local colleges and libraries in America, Italy, and Germany.

Former guards, like Thomas Todaro and Peter A. Pulia, Sr., also shared their memories in interviews and photos. Some, like Ralph Storm, wrote books about their experiences with POWs.

Even today, I receive email from the children and grandchildren of former POWs to learn more about the experiences of being a POW in the U.S. and the hope of locating records regarding their work, health, and transfers. Most of these former POWs do not or did not talk about their experiences. Mario Turrini only told his children that Hawaii was nice, with no comment on his service in Greece, Tunisia, or his experiences at the

This photo was taken at the 2009 reunion at Camp Hereford (TX). The U.S. Army is on the left, the former POWs center, and the Italian Air Force on the right. Photo by John Saffell of these men in front of the Chapel built by Italian POWs.

A belt buckle and lariat created for a reunion at Camp Atlanta (NE). (*Courtesy of Gary Reeves collection of POW artifacts*)

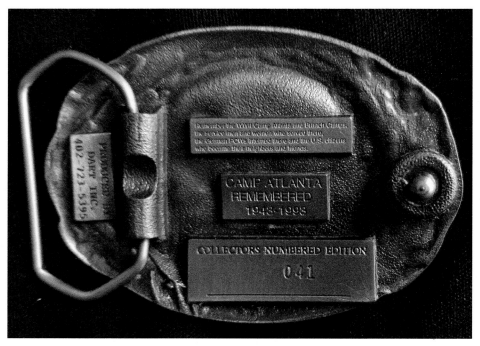

The organization of Former POWs in Italy used their old POW ID photos on their membership cards. These groups arranged reunions in Italy and at their former camps in America. Vincenzo Lo Giudice's card was provided by his daughter, Carmelina.

Above: Photo of TV interview of Joe Giordana and Gene Miconi about their POW years in Utah ASF Depot. (*Courtesy of Special Collections Department, Stewart Library, Weber State University*)

Right: Wilson Longo (named for Woodrow Wilson) was born and died in Bellosguardo, Italy. He was a prisoner at Utah ASF Depot. His cousin, Barbara, provided this photo and information.

other camps where he was held in the U.S.

Some of these letters come from Italy, but some also come from England, Australia, and the United States where these men took their families after the war.

These memories can assist us in planning for the future, promoting the preservation of photos and artifacts from the POW camps. Preservation of these memories can also be achieved by conducting interviews of surviving former POWs, their guards, and members of the community.

We can use these memories and memorabilia to educate public about the policies and experiences of WWII and to promote the good treatment of future POWs.

Mary Ravarino with photos and letters from the Italian POWs from Utah ASF Depot, who worked on her family's farm in Salt Lake City area. (*Courtesy of Italian Center of the West, UtahCulturalNews.com*)

POW Camps by Location

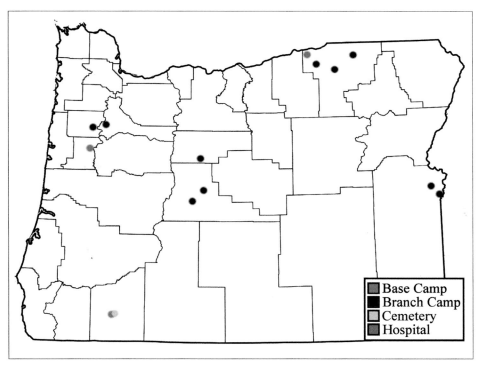

Map showing POW camps and hospitals in Oregon. (*Courtesy of John Saffell*)

There were 1,204 prisoner of war camps, Italian Service Unit camps, and prisoner of war hospitals in the U.S.

The camp lists at NARA shows several APO addresses in place of camp names. Judging by the dates, these were located in the Philippines, Hawaii, and New Caledonia.

In Oregon, there were over 5,800 German, over 850 Italian, and no Japanese POWs in thirteen POW camps and hospitals as follows:

Abbot (Camp Henry L.), Sunriver, Deschutes County, OR (branch camp under Rupert, ID). It was opened as a POW camp in June 1944. Most of site is now Sunriver Resort, with the remainder incorporated into the Deschutes National Forest. The sole remaining building from Camp Abbot is the officers' mess hall, now used for large conferences at the resort. Camp Abbot (Images of America) by Tor Hanson contains many photos of this camp.

Adair (Camp Henry R.), Corvallis, Benton and Linn Counties, OR (base camp, formerly a branch camp under Hill Field, UT. The camp opened in July 1944 for military work. The maximum Italian POW population was 234 in August 1944. The maximum German POW population was 1,305 in August 1945. It was deactivated in 1946.

Athena, Umatilla County, OR (branch camp under White). The camp opened in June 1944. The maximum population of German POWs was 250 in June 1945.

Bend, Deschutes County, OR (branch camp under Rupert, ID). The camp opened in June 1944. The maximum population of Italian POWs was 200 in June 1944.

Independence, Polk and Marion Counties, OR (branch camp under Rupert, ID). The camp opened in September 1945. The maximum population was 249 German POWs in September 1945.

Nyssa, Malheur County, OR (branch camp under Rupert, ID). The camp opened in May 1945. The maximum population was 576 German POWs in September 1945, doing agricultural work.

Pendleton, Umatilla County, OR (branch camp under Lewis, WA). The camp opened in June 1945. The maximum population was 300 German POWs in June 1945.

Salem, in Polk and Marion Counties, OR (branch camp under Rupert, ID). The camp opened in September 1945. The maximum population was 250 German POWs in September 1945.

Squaw Creek, Scotland County, OR (branch camp under Lewis, WA). The camp opened in June 1945. The maximum population was 300 German POWs in June 1945 doing agricultural work.

Stanfield, Umatilla County, OR (branch camp under White). The camp opened in June 1944. The maximum population was 250 German POWs in June 1944.

Umatilla Ordnance Depot, Umatilla County, OR (base camp) (now U.S. Army Depot). The camp opened in September 1945. The maximum population was 217 Italian Service Unit men in September 1945. It is an active military installation.

Vale, Malheur County, OR (branch camp under Rupert, ID). The camp opened in June 1945. The maximum population was 340 German POWs in June 1945 doing agricultural work.

White (Camp), near Medford, Jackson County, OR (base camp). The camp opened in May 1944. The maximum population was 2,010 German POWs in June 1944, doing work classified as military, probably just maintaining the grounds and building, perhaps building barracks for themselves, but it is most likely that some of them were also contracted out to local farmers for agricultural work. Post-war, it became White City Industrial Park and was renamed White City in 1960.

In Washington, there were over 11,800 German, nearly 2,300 Italian, and sixteen Japanese POWs in twenty POW camps and hospitals, plus one Federal prison as follows:

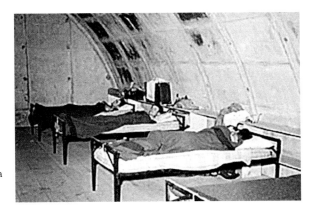

These barracks were the first built in an igloo and housed POWs at Umatilla Ordnance Depot. (*Courtesy of Library of Congress*)

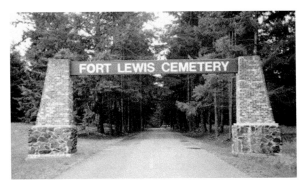

Right: Fort Lewis entrance.

Below: Map showing POW camps and hospitals in Washington. (*Courtesy of John Saffell*)

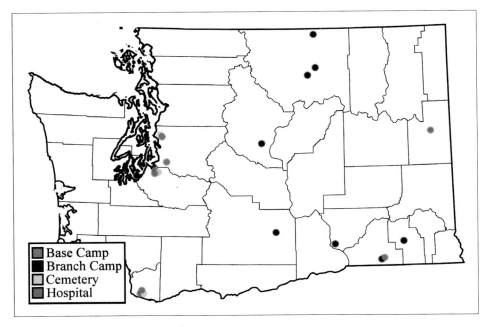

Auburn H + R Point, Auburn, King and Pierce Counties, WA (base camp). The camp opened in September 1945. The maximum population was 112 Italian Service Unit members in September 1945.

Barnes General Hospital, Vancouver Barracks, Clark County, WA (branch camp under Lewis), became an annex to the Portland Veterans Administration Medical Center. The POW camp there opened in April 1945. The maximum population of German POW workers (not patients) was thirty-two in April 1945. The maximum population of Italian Service Unit members (not patients) was 187 in September 1945. The work was classified as military because they worked on the grounds and in the hospital providing support services for the military.

Baxter (Jedediah H.) General Hospital, Spokane, Spokane County, WA, was closed in 1956 and most of the buildings demolished. In 1964, the Spokane Veterans Affairs Memorial Hospital was built and has since expanded. The POW camp there opened in April 1945. The maximum population of German POW workers was ninety-seven in April 1945, with one German patient in August 1945. The work was classified as military as in the previous entry.

Dayton, Columbia County, WA (branch camp under Lewis). The camp opened in June 1944. The maximum population was 330 German POWs in July 1944.

Lawton (Fort Henry W.), Seattle, King County, WA (base camp). The POW camp opened in March 1945. The maximum population of German POWs was 1916 in July 1945. This does not count the Italian POWs housed here temporarily awaiting transport to POW camps in Hawaii. The work was classified as military, probably for upkeep of the fort; they probably also worked on the local farms and orchards. It was closed in 2011. Fort Lawton Historic District is in Discovery Park (owned by the city of Seattle) and contains numerous historic buildings as well as the cemetery.

Lewis (Fort Meriwether), Pierce and Thurston Counties, WA (base camp) (see Spanaway). This POW camp opened in March 1944. The maximum population was 6,466 German POWs in August 1945, doing work classified as military, probably agricultural work locally while awaiting transportation home. It merged with McChord AFB in 2010 and is an active military installation.

Madigan (Patrick S.) General Hospital, Fort Lewis, Pierce County, WA (base camp), now Madigan Army Medical Center. The POW camp opened in July 1944. The maximum population was forty-nine Italian POW patients in September 1945, thirty-one German POW patients in August 1945, and fifteen Japanese POW patients in September 1945.

Malott, Okanogan County, WA (branch camp under Lewis). The camp opened in October 1944. The maximum population was 611 German POWs in October 1944 doing agricultural work.

McCaw (Walter D.) General Hospital, Walla Walla, Walla Walla County, WA (branch camp under Lewis). The POW camp opened in April 1945. The maximum population was fifty-two German POW workers (not patients) in September 1945, working at or around the hospital, so classified as military. The hospital closed in 1945, but some of the buildings were moved across the road to the veterans' hospital.

McNeil Island, Pierce County, WA. This Federal Prison acquired one Japanese POW as a prisoner in March 1946. It was transferred to Washington State Department of Corrections in 1981 and closed in 2011.

Mount Rainier Ordnance Depot, Tacoma, Pierce County, WA (base camp). This POW camp housed 223 Italian Service Unit members who worked there in September 1945. In 1962, it shifted from an Ordnance Depot to a Logistics Center for the Army and is an active military installation today.

Okanogan, Okanogan County, WA (branch camp under Lewis). This camp opened in September 1945 with a maximum population of 350 German POWs.

Oroville, Okanogan County, WA (branch camp under Lewis). This camp opened in September 1945 with a maximum population of 250 German POWs.

Pasco Engineer Depot, Pasco, Franklin County, WA. This location is listed on the ISU locations roster, but no numbers or dates are available since ISU was not part of the POW population and are not included in those population lists.

Pasco H & R Point, Pasco, Franklin County, WA. Same explanation as above.

Peshastin, Chelan County, WA (branch camp under Lewis). This POW camp opened in October 1944 with a maximum population of 431 German POWs. Today, the site has two buildings that appear to be the right age, but the owners have requested that I do not post photos and deny that the buildings were used during WWII. Local citizens remember the POW camp at that location and the buildings there used as a mess hall while the men slept in tents. This is consistent with temporary agricultural camps housing POWs. The population lists state that the work was agricultural.

Seattle ASF Depot, Seattle, King County, WA (base camp). The POW camp opened in September 1945 with a maximum population of 724 Italian Service Unit members. The work would have been in the warehouses working with military supplies.

Seattle Port of Embarkation, Seattle, King County, WA (see Vancouver Barracks). The POW camp opened in July 1944 with a maximum population of 1,000 Italian POWs. Closed in 2011, although a portion was preserved by the National Park Service as part of the Fort Vancouver National Historic Site.

Spanaway (Camp), Pierce County, WA (see Lewis)

Toppenish, Yakima County, WA (branch camp under Lewis). This camp opened in April 1945. The maximum population was 650 German POWs in July 1945 doing agricultural work.

Vancouver Barracks, Vancouver, Clark County, WA (branch camp under Lewis) (see Seattle Port of Embarkation)

Walla Walla, Walla Walla County, WA (branch camp under Lewis). This camp opened in June 1944. The maximum population was 650 German POWs in June 1945 doing agricultural work.

Death Index

A total of 880 Germans (includes three Russians, four Austrians, one Yugoslavian, one Czech and one Turk), 172 Italians, twenty-three Japanese (including one Korean) out of 1,076 POWs who died while held in the U.S. during WWI & WWII. Some ten men died or were buried in Oregon and Washington while POWs.

Biambick, Burbien was born about 1903. He died on September 28, 1945 and was buried at Vancouver Barracks, WA.

Dioguardi, Vincenzo was born in 1909. He died on December 22, 1945, and was buried at Vancouver Barracks, WA.

Elisbaraschwili, Elisabar was born in 1902. He died on August 6, 1945, and was buried on December 10 at Vancouver Barracks, WA. He was married to Tasia Elisbaraschwili.

Leonhardt, Friedrich was born January 17, 1900, in Zwickau. He died on April 17, 1945, of septicemia and was buried at Camp White, OR. His body was transferred to Vancouver Barracks Post Cemetery, WA.

Marquardt, Albert was born June 29, 1907, in Klein Sittkeim. He died October 1, 1945, in Seattle and was buried at Fort Lawton, WA. His wife was Meta Marquardt.

Messner, Kurt was born May 11, 1908 at Greifswald. He died on August 18, 1945, and was buried at Fort Lewis, WA. He was a doctor and a son of Dr. Adolph Messner.

Olivotto, Guglielmo was born in 1912. He died on August 14, 1944, in Seattle and was buried at Fort Lawton, WA.

Paluczkiewicz, Leo was born July 30, 1917, in Duisburg. He died on July 4, 1945, at Walla Walla and was buried at Fort Lewis, WA. His mother was Maria.

Planker, Jakob was born October 16, 1906, in Krefeld. He died on August 3, 1945, and was buried at Camp White, OR. His body was transferred to Vancouver Barracks Post Cemetery, WA.

Simon, Karl was born December 28, 1923, in Garmisch Partenkirchen. He died on January 20, 1945, in Tacoma and was buried at Fort Lewis, WA. His father was Franz Dehmer.

Burial Locations List

A total of ninety-one U.S. Military and civilian cemeteries contained POW burials in the United States.

Oregon: Camp White, OR (two German WWII POW burials transferred to Vancouver Barracks Post Cemetery, WA)

Washington: Fort Lawton Post Cemetery, WA, now within Discovery Park, Seattle, WA but owned and maintained by the U.S. Army Reserve. The cemetery contains one Italian and one German POW burial and is open to the public.

Fort Lewis Post Cemetery, WA, an active military installation. The cemetery contains three German WWII POW burials.

Vancouver Barracks Post Cemetery, WA, Federal land. The cemetery contains two German and one Italian WWII POW burials, plus two German POW burials transferred from OR. This cemetery is currently run by the Vancouver Barracks Military Association and open to the public. Contract the through vbma.us/projectsCemetery.html or president@vbma.us.

Appendix A

POW Labor

POW work images. (*PMGO, located at NARA College Park, MD, RG 389*)

PRISONERS OF WAR WORK

CLOTHING AND EQUIPMENT

FORT MEADE, MD.

CAMP BLANDING, FLA.

FORT McCLELLAN, ALA.

CAMP BRECKINRIDGE, KY.

FORT OGELTHORPE, GA.

CAMP CARSON, COLO.

WD – ASF – PMGO

MAN-MONTHS SUMMARY OF PRISONER-OF-WAR LABOR

A man-months (strength) summary of prisoner-of-war labor availability, assignment to paid work, and type of work performed, are given in the table and chart below. These data are for all prisoners in the United States except those in Italian Service Units, penal and medical institutions, and Hawaii. Man-months of prisoners available for paid work and prisoners at work are calculated by dividing the total number of man-days so reported by the number of workdays in the month. These man-months data represent average prisoner strength for the month.

MAN-MONTHS OF PRISONER-OF-WAR LABOR, BY TYPE OF WORK AND BY MONTH,
NOVEMBER AND DECEMBER 1944, AND JANUARY AND FEBRUARY 1945

Item	Nov 1944	Dec 1944	Jan 1945	Feb 1945
AVAILABILITY AND ASSIGNMENT				
TOTAL MAN-MONTHS a/	306,542	318,034	316,824	318,562
NOT AVAILABLE FOR PAID WORK	95,181	89,862	95,806	95,681
AVAILABLE FOR PAID WORK	211,361	228,172	221,018	222,881
Not Assigned to Work	25,564	34,392	30,074	23,819
Assigned to Work	185,797	193,780	190,944	199,062
Work Stoppage b/	16,273	22,020	19,139	18,559
Worked Full Time	169,524	171,760	171,805	180,503
TYPE OF PAID WORK				
TOTAL MAN-MONTHS	169,524	171,760	171,805	180,503
Prisoner-of-War Camp Work	27,212	28,975	27,810	28,090
Army Post, Camp, and Station Work . . .	85,281	96,915	102,831	112,711
Contract Work	57,031	45,870	41,164	39,702

a/ Calculated from total man-days. Excludes prisoners of war in Italian Service Units, penal and medical institutions, and the Territory of Hawaii.
b/ Average number of men assigned to work but idle each workday during the month because of bad weather, non-use by contract employer, and other temporary causes of work stoppage.

MAN-MONTHS AVAILABLE FOR LABOR, AND TYPE OF WORK DONE BY PRISONERS OF WAR*

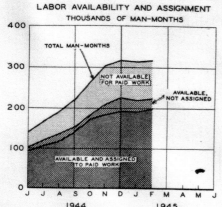

LABOR AVAILABILITY AND ASSIGNMENT
THOUSANDS OF MAN-MONTHS

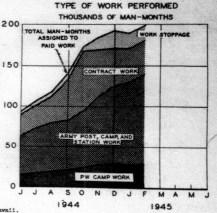

TYPE OF WORK PERFORMED
THOUSANDS OF MAN-MONTHS

* Excludes prisoners in Italian Service Units, institutions, and Hawaii.

PRISONERS OF WAR WORK

MOTOR MAINTENANCE

FT. DIX, N. J.

FORT ROBINSON, NEB.

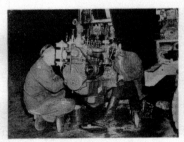

FORT KNOX, KY.

FORT DIX, N. J.

CAMP CAMPBELL, KY.

FT. BRAGG, N. C.

WD - ASF - PMGO

PRISONERS OF WAR WORK

REPAIRS AND UTILITIES

FOLLOWING LIST OF SUGGESTED REPAIRS AND UTILITIES OCCUPATIONS FOR PRISONERS OF WAR WAS PREPARED BY OFFICE OF THE
CHIEF OF ENGINEERS

SPECIFICATION NUMBER   OCCUPATION
(TM. E - 427)

CAMP CLARK, MO.

FORT OGELTHORPE, GA.

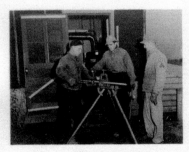

CAMP CLARK, MO.

FORT LEONARD WOOD, MO.

WD – ASF – PM GO

TAILOR, CLOTHING REPAIR SHOP

COBBLERS, SHOE REPAIR SHOP

MECHANIC, TYPEWRITER REPAIR SHOP

OCCUPATIONS AND SKILLS OF

PRISONERS OF WAR

Auto body repairmen
Auto painters
Auto mechanics
Artists
Bakers, bread and pastry
   Mixers
   Oven operators
   Moulders
   Dividers
Barbers
Blacksmiths
Bookkeepers
Boot and shoe repairmen
Boxmakers
Bricklayers
Brushmen
Bulldozer operators
Butchers
Cabinetmakers
Canvas workers
Carpenters
   Bench
   Car
   Concrete form
   House
   Rough
Car washers and greasers
Cement and concrete
   finishers
Ceramic workers
Checkers
Chemists
   Sewage disposal plant
Cleaners
   Engine
   Floor
   Machine
Clerks
   General office
   Statistical
   Stock
Clothing classifiers
Clothing repairmen
Coal handlers
Cobblers
Countermen
Concrete workers
Construction machinery
   operators
Construction laborers
Cooks
   EM mess
   Officers' mess
   PX restaurant
Coppersmiths
Cranemen
Craters
Dairymen
Dental lab. workers
Ditch diggers
Draftsmen
Dragline operators
Dyers
Electrical repairmen

Electricians
   Auto
   House
   Motor
   Radio
Engravers
Fan cleaners
Farm hands
Farm machinery operators
Firemen
   Boiler and furnace
   Fire department
Form builders
Flashlight repairmen
Freight handlers
Furnace cleaners
Furnace tenders
Furniture repairmen
Foundry workers
Garbage laborers
Garbage collectors
Gardners
Glaziers
Goldsmiths
Graders and packers
   Fruit and vegetable
Grass mowers
Grave diggers
Greenhouse workers
Grounds keepers
Harness makers
Harvest hands
   Cotton
   Fruit
   General
   Sugar beets
   Sugarcane
   Tobacco
   Vegetable
Hospital orderlies
Incinerator operators
Insect exterminators
Interpreters
Instrument repairmen
Irrigation workers
Janitors
Jewelers
Kitchen police
Laborer, general
Language teachers
Latrine orderlies
Laundry workers
   Checker
   Marker
   Presser
   Sorter
   Washer
Leather workers
Locksmiths
Lumberyard workers
Machinists
Masons
Meatcutters
Mechanics

OCCUPATIONS AND SKILLS OF

PRISONERS OF WAR (Continued)

Maintenance workers:
 Ditches
 Grounds
 Powerline right-of-way
 Railroad right-of-way
 Roads and streets
 Septic tanks
Model and pattern makers
Molders
Motor repairmen
 Electrical
 Gasoline and diesel
Nurserymen
Office-machine repairmen
Oilers
Orthopedic aids
Painters
 Construction
 Maintenance
 Vehicle
Paper balers
Photograph finishers
Photographers' assistants
Physicians
Piano tuners
Pinboys
Plasterers
Printers
Plumbers
Poultry dressers
Pulpwood cutters
Quarry workers
Radio repairmen
Ration breakdown workers
Repairmen
 Automobile
 Clothing
 Electrical
 Furniture
 Instrument
 Motor
 Office machine
 Radio
 Road equipment
 Shoe
 Tent
 Tire
 Typewriter
 Watch
Railroad maintenance
 workers
Refrigeration mechanics
Road equipment repairmen
Roofers
Salvage workers:
 Building materials
 Clothing and equipment
 Electrical equipment
 Motors
 Paper
Sew filers
Sawmill workers
Scrubmen
Servicemen, motor pool
Sheet metal workers

Sewage disposal plant
 operators
Shoe classifiers
Shoe repairmen
Sign painters
Silversmiths
Spray operators
 Mosquito control
 Tree spraying
Stablemen
Steam cleaners
 Vehicles
Steam fitters
Stonecutters
Stone masons
Storekeepers
Sweepers
Tailors
Teachers
Teamsters
Telephone linemen
Tent repairmen
Textile balers
Tile setters
Timekeepers
Tinsmiths
Tire changers
Tire repairmen
Tool checkers and sorters
Tool dressers and
 sharpeners
Track repairmen
Tree fallers
Tractor drivers
Truck drivers
Type setters
Typewriter repairmen
Typists
Upholsterers
 Furniture
 Vehicles
Veterinarians
Waiters
 EM mess
 Officers' club
 PX restaurant
Ward boys
 Station hospital
Warehousemen
 Post ordnance
 Post quartermaster
 Salvage shop
 Post exchange
 Private industry
Wash-rack man
Watch repairmen
Water plant operators
Weavers
 Basketry
Webbing repairmen
Welders
Woodsmen
Wood workers
X-ray lab. technicians
Yardmen

MECHANICS, VEHICLE REPAIR SHOP

AUTO PAINTER, VEHICLE REPAIR SHOP

PLUMBERS, POST PLUMBING SHOP

PRISONERS OF WAR WORK

POST ENGINEER WORK

CAMP TRINIDAD, COLO.

CAMP SHELBY, MISS.

FORT LEONARD WOOD, MO.

CAMP BRECKINRIDGE, KY.

CAMP BRECKINRIDGE, KY.

CAMP WHEELER, GA.

WD - ASF - PMGO

PRISONERS OF WAR WORK

POST ENGINEER WORK

CAMP CLINTON, MISS.

CAMP SUTTON, N. C.

EDGEWOOD ARSENAL, MD.

CAMP CARSON, COLO.

GALVESTON AAB, TEX.

FORT LEONARD WOOD, MO.

WD – ASF – PMGO

PRISONERS OF WAR WORK

POST ENGINEER WORK

FORT BENJAMIN HARRISON, IND.

CAMP BRECKINRIDGE, KY.

NORFOLK ARMY AIR BASE, VA.

CAMP CLINTON, MISS.

FORT DEVENS, MASS.

CAMP LEE, VA.

WD - ASF - PMGO

INSTRUCTIONS TO THE CONTRACTOR
UNDER CONTRACT FOR PRISONER OF WAR LABOR

The treatment and employment of prisoners of war are governed by an
international treaty called the Geneva Convention. The United States
Government is bound to follow the terms of this treaty. It is also
important to do so, and to treat enemy prisoners fairly, in order to
avoid appraisals against American Prisoners held by enemy countries. As a
contractor using prisoner of war labor you have agreed and are required
to obey the provisions of the Geneva Convention. You have also agreed and
are required to comply with War Department security regulations relative
to prisoners of war. The following instructions have been prepared for
your guidance.

1 In case of any escape or unwarranted conduct on the part of any
prisoner of war, you should inform the guard detail commander in charge of
the prisoners, who is responsible for their conduct. You should make you
telephone available to him so that he may phone the camp commander at any
time.

2 You should not fraternize with prisoners of war or allow third persons
to do so. If you fraternize with them, and there is an escape, your action
might tend to make it appear you had helped in the escape. Helping a
prisoner of war to escape is a serious criminal offense.

3 In addition to precautions taken by the guards, you should exercise
every reasonable care that prisoners of war do not escape from your
premises. You should cooperate fully with the military authorities and
guards in the matter of taking steps to avoid escapes.

4 You should not allow prisoners to wear clothing other than that
issued by the War Department. Their clothing has been marked to identify
them as prisoners of war. Do not give them old hats or coats to wear.

5 You should fully occupy the time of the prisoners. If a situation
arises where they cannot work, notify the guard detail commander so the
prisoners can be returned to camp instead of being idle around your premises.

6 All prisoner of war mail, even to persons in the United States, must
be censored. Therefore it is very important that you cooperate fully
with the guard detail commander in preventing any prisoner from mailing
letters, cards, packages or cards from your premises, and in preventing
third persons who might smuggle mail from mixing with the prisoners.
Prisoners must not make telephone calls or send cables or telegrams. You
should report to the guard detail commander any violations of this rule.

7 The guard detail commander is responsible that only authorized newspaper reporters, news photographers or newsreel cameramen attempt to
secure information or photographs the prisoners of war. You must
cooperate with the guard in this respect. You yourself should
not give out any publicity regarding the prisoners of war.

POW contract instructions. (*Courtesy of
Gary Reeves collection of POW artifacts*)

8. You do not need workmen's compensation insurance for the benefit
of the prisoners of war performing work under your contract. This
matter is covered by War Department regulations.

9. Your civilian employees and others who may come in contact with
the prisoners of war in the performance of the contract should be
informed of these instruction and should be enjoined to carry them out.

10. The War Department expects your cooperation in these matters so
that the prisoner of war labor program will be successful. Failure
on your part to follow these instructions, and other instructions given
you by the military authorities, may result in cancellation of the
contract and refusal of the War Department to furnish prisoner of
war labor to you in the future.

11. The Government reserves the right to supplement or change these
instructions. These instructions do not in any way modify or limit
your obligations under the contract.

12. This bulletin should be posted in such places in or around your
establishment so that these instructions may be known to all civilian
personnel employed by you.

SUPPLEMENT "A"

1a. It is your responsibility to furnish all supervision necessary
for the efficient operation of any prisoner of war detail. Guards are
responsible for the safe guarding of prisoners of war and should not be
expected to direct prisoner of war labor for the contractor.

2a. You should refrain from taking any disciplinary action regarding
prisoners of war, as no prisoner of war can be forced to work. Need
for any disciplinary action should be reported to the guard, and his
instructions should be followed.

3a. Always remember that the way you treat prisoners of war
determines the treatment given American soldiers who are prisoners of
war in German hands.

Hq. 1663rd SU Form No. 33

ARMY SERVICE FORCES
HEADQUARTERS, SIXTH SERVICE COMMAND
Chicago 6, Illinois

6 May 1944

In Reply Refer To: SPJIP 383.6

To: All Law Enforcement Agencies,
States of Illinois, Michigan, and Wisconsin

During the coming summer months, it is contemplated to have German prisoners of war working on various agricultural projects in the States of Illinois, Michigan, and Wisconsin, and it is with the thought of a possible escape from one of these projects, that the following is given for your official information and not general publication:

I. Prisoners of war are in the custody of the War Department and their treatment as prisoners of war is covered by the Geneva Convention of 1929. Germany and the United States are both subscribers to this Convention and the treatment that is accorded German prisoners of war in this country is reflected in the treatment accorded Americans held as prisoners of war by the German Government. The Geneva Convention is reproduced by the Government Printing Office, Washington, D.C., and can be obtained for a nominal fee.

II. Prisoners of war are not prisoners in the commonly accepted usage of that term by law enforcement officers. Neither are they fugitives from justice. Unless, in an escapee status, they violate some civil law of the United States, State or municipality, they should be treated as honorable soldiers. Prisoners of war, unless guilty of some civil offense, should not be handcuffed or placed in common cells. If apprehended by civil authorities, they should be restrained under guard until they can be turned over to the nearest military authorities. Experience develops that German prisoners will be found to be amenable to authority and very unlikely to offer any resistance to arrest.

III. Prisoners of war have a legal right to attempt to escape and it may be assumed at all times that they will endeavor to attempt to escape if the opportunity presents itself. As members of the armed forces of the enemy, they may be expected to have a constant, fixed intention to advance as much as possible the aims and aspirations of their country. They may also be expected to attempt to communicate with enemy sympathizers, to acquire and transmit information of military value or to cause damage, delay, or other acts to deter our war effort.

IV. (A) Articles of the U. S. Army uniform are not issued unless altered in a manner that will prevent them from being mistaken for parts of the Army uniform, such as, removing all official buttons on all undyed articles of the U.S. Army uniform, and replacing them with buttons, bone or

POW labor in Sixth Service Command. (*Courtesy of Gary Reeves collection of POW artifacts*)

SPJIP 383.6, 6 May 1944 (Continued)

VI. Your cooperation in giving assistance when requests are made by representatives of the War Department, in connection with the operation of prisoner of war "Labor Details", will be appreciated.

W. E. GUTHNER
Brigadier General, G.S.C.
Director
Security and Intelligence Division

Work contracts for civilians to obtain POW labor.
(*Courtesy of Michael Pomeroy*)

Appendix B

Museums and Websites

Arizona Historical Society Museum, Papago Park, AZ: arizonahistoricalsociety.org/museums

Benton County Historical Museum, 1101 Main St., Philomath, OR: bentoncountymuseum.org

Billion Graves: billiongraves.com

Bureau of Land Management, Needles, CA: blm.gov/tag/needles-field-office

California Military Museum, militarymuseum.org, aka the California State Military Museum, 28th and B streets, Sacramento, CA.

Camp Aliceville: encyclopediaofalabama.org/face/Article.isp?id-2322.

Camp Hearne Museum: camphearne.com/index.htm

Camp Opelika: eastalabama.org/Exhibits/Exhibits.htm

Camp Roberts Historical Museum, Bldg. 114

Camp Roberts, CA 93451-5000 (12 miles north of Paso Robles, CA): camprobertshistoricalmuseum.com/

Camp Ruston: latech.edu/library/scma/index.php

Camp Van Dorn World War II Museum: vandorn.org

Camp White Military Museum located in the VA SORCC facility in White City, OR

Cemetery Records Online: interment.net

Deschutes County Historical Museum, 129 NW Idaho Ave, Bend, OR 97703: deschuteshistory.org

Door County Maritime Museum, Sturgeon Bay, WI has display on WWII POWs in the area orchards

Drew County Museum, Monticello, AR has a display on WWII POWs at Camp Monticello.

Eastern California Museum, Lone Pine, CA: inyocounty.us/ecmsite/

Family Search: familysearch.org

Find a Grave: findagrave.com

Fort Douglas, Salt Lake City, UT: fortdouglas.org/about/virtual-tour, also cemetery

Fort George G. Meade Museum: ftmeade.army.mil/museum/Museum_POW.html

Fort Leonard Wood Museum: visitmo.com/museums-at-fort-leonard-wood.aspx

Fort Lewis Military Museum: lewisarmymuseum.com/, the museum is accessible to the public without a visitor's pass. To gain access, please follow the instructions as follows

1. Take Exit 119 off of I-5
2. Turn right onto Dupont-Steilacoom Rd
3. Turn right at the gate (first right beyond small commercial area and hotel) and follow the gravel road up to the parking lot.
4. Park in the parking lot and call the museum by cell phone at 253-967-7206.
5. You will be escorted through the gate to the museum on foot.

GenTracer—World War II: gentracer.org

German War Graves Commission: volksbund.de

Library of Congress: catalog.loc.gov

March Field Air Museum, Riverside, CA: marchfield.org

Mississippi Armed Forces Museum, Camp Shelby, MS: armedforcesmuseum.us/Pages/Newsletter.pdf

Mountain Empire Historical Society and Stone Museum, Campo, CA: cssmus.org/

Oregon Historical Society Davies Family Research Library, Portland, OR 97205 has eighty-one photos from the U.S. Army Signal Corps in their archives.

Palm Springs Air Museum, Palm Springs, CA: palmspringsairmuseum.org/

General George S. Patton Memorial Museum, Chiriaco Summit, CA: generalpattonmuseum.com/

Traces: www.traces.org

Tracy Historical Museum, 1141 Adams St., Tracy, CA

U.K. National Archives: www.nationalarchives.gov.uk

U.S. Dept. of Veterans Affairs National Cemeteries: www.cem.va.gov/cem/cems/listcem.asp

U.S. National Archives and Records Administration: www.archives.gov

U.S. National Park Service: www.nps.gov

Weber State University, Stewart Library, Special Collections Exhibits, "Prisoners of War in Ogden" at library.weber.edu/collections/special_collections

Bibliography

Adams, Meredith Lentz. "A Miscarriage of Justice?" interview by Jim Kelly. Sunflower Journeys Home 16101A. KTWU. 2003.
_____. *Murder and Martial Justice: Spying and Retribution in World War II America*. Kent, Ohio: Kent State University Press, 2011.
_____. "The Abortive Attempt to Exchange GI and German POWs". (Presentation, TRACES conference, May 31, 2003).

Alberts, Betty. Interview by author. March 10, 2012.

Amdt, Karl John Richard. "German P.O.W. Camp Papers." Microfilm. Washington, DC: Library of Congress Photo-duplication Service, 1965. Library of Congress. lccn.loc.gov/83125121.

Angerilli, Adriano. Interview by author. August 14 ,2009.

Army Service Forces. "Service Command Operating Personnel and Prisoners, 31 March 1945", NARA RG 389, Entry 261, Box 2563. National Archives at College Park, College Park, MD.

Bland, John Paul. *Secret War at Home: The Pine Grove Furnace Prisoner of War Interrogation Camp*. Cumberland County Historical Society, Carlisle, PA, 2006.

Boni, Andrea. Interview by author. November 3, 2018.

Boudreaux, Henry J, Capt., C.M.P. Report of Investigation of the deaths of Leonello Bini, Vito Clemente, Adolfo Nitri, Antonino Paleologo, July 21, 1943, NARA RG 389, Entry 461, Box 2562. National Archives at College Park, College Park, MD.

Bryan, B.M., Brigadeer General. Assistant Provost Marshal General, Letter to Army Services Forces regarding transfer of POWs, August 26, 1944, NARA RG 389, Entry 457, Box 1419. National Archives at College Park, College Park, MD.

Bulkat, Ernst. Interview by author. March 11, 2007.

Bykofsky, Joseph and Harold Larson. *United States Army in World War II: The Technical Services: The Transportation Corps: Operations Overseas*. Center of Military History, United States Army, Washington, DC, 2003.

Carlson, Lewis. "POW Experience: Myth and Reality". (Presentation, TRACES conference, 6 October 2002).

Conn, Stetson and Byron Fairchild. *The United States Army in World War II, The Western Hemisphere, The Framework of Hemisphere Defense*. Washington, DC: Office of the Chief of Military History, Department of the Army, 1960.

Conn, Stetson and Rose C Engelman and Byron Fairchild, *The United States Army in World War II, The Western Hemisphere, Guarding the United States and its Outposts*. Washington, DC: Office of the Chief of Military History, Department of the Army, 1964

Corbin, Alexander, *The History of Camp Tracy: Japanese WWII POWs and the Future of Strategic Interrogation*. Fort Belvoir, VA: Ziedon Press, 2009

Cosentini, George and Norman Gruenzner. *United States Numbered Military Post Offices Assignments and Locations 1941–1994*. The Military Postal History Society, 1994.

Cowley, Betty. *Stalag Wisconsin: Inside WWII Prisoner-of-war Camps*. Oregon, WI: Badger Books, 2002.

Cunningham, Raymond Kelly. *Prisoners at Fort Douglas: War Prison Barracks Three and the alien enemies, 1917–1920*. Salt Lake City, UT: Fort Douglas Military Museum, 1983.

Daugherty, Joseph B., Col. Assistant, Office of the Quartermaster General, Letter to Provost Marshal General regarding repatriation of ISU units, dated October 9, 1945, NARA RG 389, Entry 261, Box 2563. National Archives and Records Administration, College Park, MD
_____. Letter to Provost Marshal General regarding repatriation of ISU units, dated August 28, 1945, NARA RG 389, Entry 261, Box 2563. National Archives and Records Administration, College Park, MD

"Department of Veterans Affairs National Cemeteries," United States Department of Veterans Affairs, cem.va.gov/cem/cems/listcem.asp.

Ducharme, Joseph O.C., Lt. Col. Director, Enemy PW Information Bureau, Camp Holabird, MD, to Provost Marshal General, regarding cemetery locations, dated February 16, 1953, NARA RG 389, Entry 261, Box 2562. National Archives and Records Administration, College Park, MD
_____. Regarding cemetery locations, dated February 16, 1953, NARA RG 389, Entry 467, Box 1513. National Archives and Records Administration, College Park, MD

Dvorak, Petula. "Fort Hunt's Quiet Men Break Silence on WWII: Interrogator Fought "Battle of Wits"." *The Washington Post*. October 6, 2007.

Edwards, Earl L., Lt. Col. Asst. Dir., Prisoner of War Division, Letter to Army Services Forces, regarding prisoner segregation, dated March 3, 1944, NARA RG 389, Entry 261, Box 2563. National Archives and Records Administration, College Park, MD
_____. Letter Regarding Prisoner Transfer, dated October 16, 1943, NARA RG 389, Entry 261, Box 2563. National Archives and Records Administration, College Park, MD
_____. Letter Regarding Prisoner Transfer, dated January 7, 1943, NARA RG 389, Entry 261, Box 2563. National Archives and Records Administration, College Park, MD

Enemy Prisoner of War Information Bureau. "World War II Enemy Prisoners of War Deceased in Theaters of Operations, Fort Holabird, MD, 2 July 1952", NARA RG 389, Entry 466, Box 1. National Archives and Records Administration, College Park, MD

Eppinga, Jane. *Death at Papago Park POW Camp: A Tragic Murder and America's Last Mass Execution*. Charleston, SC: The History Press, 2017.

Erichsen, Heino R. *The Reluctant Warrior: Former German POW Finds Peace in Texas*. Austin, TX: Eakin Press, 2001.

_____. Interview by author. October 7, 2002.

Fairchild, Byron and Jonathan Grossman. *United States Army in World War II: The War Department: The Army and Industrial Manpower*. Center of Military History, Department of the Army, Washington, DC, 2002.

Farrand, Stephen M. Major, Prisoner of War Operations Division, Letter to Special War Problems Division regarding the death of Karl Schaeffer, dated May 28, 1945, NARA RG 389, Entry 261, Box 2562. National Archives and Records Administration, College Park, MD

_____. Letter to Special War Problems Division regarding the death of Alfred Malinowski, dated February 20, 1945, NARA RG 389, Entry 261, Box 2562. National Archives and Records Administration, College Park, MD

"Find a Grave," Find a Grave, findagrave.com/.

Fischer, H. P., Office of the Commanding General, 9th Service Command, Fort Douglas, UT, Letter to Army Service Forces regarding new base camps, dated March 31, 1945, NARA RG 389, Entry 457, Box 1419. National Archives and Records Administration, College Park, MD

Ford, George. German Guard Held in Medical Ward After Shooting 28 Germans: Probe Opened by Army Into Salina Affair". The Deseret News, July 9, 1945.

Gansberg, Judith M., *Stalag: USA: The Remarkable Story of German POWs in America*. New York, NY: Thomas Y. Crowell Company, 1977.

German War Graves Commission at volksbund.de

Giordana, Beth. Interview by author. August 2001.

Griffith, L.E. Lt. Col., Prisoner of War Operations Division, Letter to Mrs. Ada Errera regarding transfer of body to Italy, dated April 30, 1946, NARA RG 389, Entry 261, Box 2562. National Archives and Records Administration, College Park, MD

Hamann, Jack. *On American Soil: How Justice Became a Casualty of World War II*. Algonquin Books, 2005.

Hanson, Tor. *Camp Abbot (Images of America)*. Arcadia Publishing, 2018

Heisler, Barbara Schmitter. "Returning to America: German Prisoners of War and the American Experience", German Studies Review, Vol. 31, No. 3 (Oct., 2008), pp. 537–556; Published by The Johns Hopkins University Press on behalf of the German Studies Association

Heitmann, John A. "Enemies are Human." (Presentation, Dayton Christian-Jewish Dialogue, May 10, 1998).

Iannantuoni, Mario. Interview by author. February 10, 2012.

Jensen, Carol A. *Images of America: Byron Hot Springs*. San Francisco, CA: Arcadia Publishing, 2006.

Jones, L.B.C. Lt. Col. Deputy Director, Internal Security Division, Regarding Security, dated October 14, 1943, NARA RG 389, Entry 261, Box 2563. National Archives and Records Administration, College Park, MD

Keefer, Louis E., *Italian Prisoners of War in America, 1942–1946: Captives or Allies?* New York, NY: Praeger, 1992.

Kirkpatrick, Kathy. Italian POWs in Utah." (Presentation, TRACES conference, October 7, 2002)

_____ (Presentation, TRACES conference, May 31, 2003).

Kleinman, Steven M. "The History of MIS-Y: US Strategic Interrogation During World War II". Master's thesis, Joint Military Intelligence College, 2002.

Knappe, Siegfried & Ted Brusaw. *Soldat: Reflections of a German Soldier 1936–1949*. New York, NY: Orion Books, 1992.

Krammer, Arnold. "American Treatment of German Generals" The Journal of Military History 54, No. 1 (January 1990): 27–46.

_____. "German Prisoners of War in the United States" Military Affairs 40, No. 2 (April 1976): 68–73.

_____. *Nazi Prisoners of War in America*. Lanham, MD: Scarborough House, 1996.

Leighton, Richard M., and Robert W. Coakley. *The United States Army in World War II, The War Department, Global Logistics and Strategy 1940–1943*, Washington, DC: Office of the Chief of Military History, Department of the Army, 1955.

Lewis, George G, and John Mewha. *History of Prisoner of War Utilization by the United States Army, 1776–1945*. U.S. Department of the Army, Pamphlet 20-213, Washington, DC: Government Printing Office, 1955.

L'Ufficio Informazione Vaticano per I pregionieri di guerra istituito da Pio XII, Vatican Secret Archives. Vatican City.

Lucioli, Ezio. Interview by author. August 14, 2009.

Luick-Thrams, Michael. "The Fritz Ritz: German POWs in the American Heartland" (Presentation, TRACES conference, May 31, 2003).

Margotilli, Giuseppe. Interview by author. August 14, 2009.

Martin, Charles E., Col., Director of Personnel, Memorandum to Armed Service Forces, regarding release of ISU, dated October 3, 1945, NARA RG 389, Entry 261, Box 2563. National Archives and Records Administration, College Park, MD

_____. Memorandum to Armed Service Forces, regarding release of ISU, dated August 23, 1945, NARA RG 389, Entry 261, Box 2563. National Archives and Records Administration, College Park, MD

_____. Memorandum to Armed Service Forces, regarding release of ISU, dated August 20, 1945, NARA RG 389, Entry 261, Box 2563. National Archives and Records Administration, College Park, MD

Meier, Susan Ann, "Limited Freedom: The Italian Service Units in Southern California's Inland Empire During World War II". Thesis at California State University, Fullerton: 2004

Moore, John Hammond. Italian POWs in America: War is Not Always Hell." Prologue (Fall 1976): 141–151.

_____. *Wacko War: Strange Tales from America 1941–1945*. Raleigh, NC: Pentland Press, 2001.

Nagler, Joerg A. "Enemy Aliens and Internment in World War I: Alvo von Alvensleben in Fort Douglas, Utah, a Case Study." Utah Historical Quarterly 58 (Fall 1990): 388–406

Nash, Gerald D. *The American West Transformed: The Impact of the Second World War*. Bloomington, IN: Indiana University Press, 1985.

National Archives and Records Administration, Record Group 38. Records of the Navy; Special Activities Branch (OP-16-Z), Navy Unit, Tracy, California. National Archives and Records Administration, College Park, MD

_____. Record Group 331. Records of Allied Operational and Occupation Headquarters, World War II. Entry 3A, Box 126. Repatriation to USSR. National Archives and Records Administration, College Park, MD

_____. Record Group 389. Records of the Office of the Provost Marshal General. National Archives and Records Administration, College Park, MD

Oregon, Death Index, 1903–1998," index, FamilySearch (https://familysearch.org/pal:/MM9.1.1/VZCC-CQH), Friedrich Leonhardt, 1945.

_____. Death Index, 1903–1998, index, FamilySearch (familysearch.org/pal:/MM9.1.1/VZC4-J1S), Jakob Planker, 1945.

Orsini, August. Interview by author. October 7, 2011.

Palermo, Raffaele. "ISU Personnel Records." Al Ministero della Difesa, Rome, Italy.

Parri, Dino. *Il Giuramento; Generale a El Alamein, prigioniero in America (1942–1945)*. Milano: Mursia, 2009.

"*Per il Soldato Francesco Erriquez la guerra è finita!*," *Un Mondo di Italiani*, unmondoditaliani.com/per-il-soldato-francesco-erriquez-la-guerra-e-finita.htm.

Pisani, Pat and Maria. Interview by author. June 12, 2009.

Powell, Allan Kent.*Splinters of a Nation; German Prisoners of War in Utah*. Salt Lake City, UT: University of Utah Press, 1989.

Prisoners in Paradise, DVD, directed by Camilla Calamandrei. 2001.

"Prisoners of War in Ogden: 1943–1946," Weber State University Stewart Library, library.weber.edu/asc/POW/default.cfm.

Pulia, Peter A., Sr. Interview by author. May 1, 2002.

Reiss, Matthias. "Bronzed Bodies behind Barbed Wire: Masculinity and the Treatment of German Prisoners of War in the United States during World War II." The Journal of Military History 69, No. 2 (April 2005): 475-504.

Richards, Su. Interview by author. May 23, 2009.

Rogers, John R. Interview by author. September 3, 2007.

Salgado, Rebecca C. "Rebuilding the Network: Interpretation of World War II Prisoner-of-War Camps in the United States." Master's Thesis, Columbia University, May 2012.

Scott, Ralph. "Violations of International Law in the Treatment of German POWs Following the Cessation of Hostilities". (Presentation, TRACES conference, June 1, 2003).

Selmi, Andrea. Interview by author. November 2, 2018.

Smith, Clarence McKittrick. *United States Army in World War II: The Technical Services: The Medical Department: Hospitalization and Evacuation, Zone of Interior*. Center of Military History, United States Army, Washington, DC, 2003.

Spidle, Jake W. Jr. "Axis Prisoners of War in the United States, 1942-1946: A Bibliographical Essay." Military Affairs 39, No. 2 (April 1975): 61–66.

"State Department-Related Sites: Hotels and Resorts," German American Internee Coalition, gaic.info/ShowPage.php?section=Internment_Camps_

Storm, Ralph A., *Camp Florence Days*. N.p. 2007.

Thomas, Jennie M. "History of the Prisoner of War Camp Utah ASF Depot, Ogden, UT", February 1, 1945.

Thompson, Antonio S., *Men in German Uniform: POWs in America during World War II*, Knoxville, TN: University of Tennessee Press, 2010.

Tissing, Robert Warren Jr. "Utilization of Prisoners of War in the United States During World War II: Texas, A Case Study". Master's Thesis, Baylor University, 1973.

Todaro, Robert J. Interview by author. June 12, 2006.

Togni, Fernando. Interview by author. August 14, 2009.

Tollefson, A.M., Col., Director, Prisoner of War Operations, Letter to Special Projects Division regarding the death of Giovanni Cincotta, dated January 10, 1946, NARA RG 389, Entry 462, Box 2562. National Archives and Records Administration, College Park, MD

_____. Letter to Special Projects Division regarding the death of Giovanni E. Bondini, dated June 8, 1945, NARA RG 389, Entry 261, Box 2562. National Archives and Records Administration, College Park, MD

_____. Letter to Special Projects Division regarding Salina shooting, dated August 28, 1945, NARA RG 389, Entry 261, Box 2562. National Archives and Records Administration, College Park, MD

Trezzani, Claudio. Letter from Monticello PW Camp, AR, dated January 26, 1944. Stato Maggiore Esercito, #2256A, Rome, Italy

Turrini, Marcello. Interview by author. November 22, 2016.

Ulio, J.A., Major General, the Adjutant General's office, letter to The Commanding Generals, dated April 9, 1943. NARA RG 389, Entry 261, Box 2563. National Archives and Records Administration, College Park, MD

University of Utah. *Historic Fort Douglas at the University of Utah, a Brief History & Walking Tour*, Salt Lake City, UT: University of Utah, 2000.

Urwiller, Clifford S., Col. Prisoner of War Operations Division, Memorandum for Camp Operations Branch regarding surplus ISU units, dated October 18, 1945, NARA RG 389, Entry 261, Box 2563. National Archives and Records Administration, College Park, MD

_____. Memorandum for Camp Operations Branch regarding surplus ISU units, dated September 14, 1945, NARA RG 389, Entry 261, Box 2563. National Archives and Records Administration, College Park, MD

U.S. House. Report of Committee on Military Affairs. 78th Congress., 2nd sess., H. Res. 30.

U.S. House. Report of Committee on Military Affairs. 79th Congress., 1st sess., H. Res. 20.

Vecchio, Giovanni and Orazio. Interview by author. November 17, 2018.

War Department, to Commanding Generals, Regarding movement orders, dated November 14, 1945, NARA RG 389, Entry 261, Box 2563. National Archives and Records Administration, College Park, MD

_____. Regarding movement orders, dated November 1, 1945, NARA RG 389, Entry 261, Box 2563. National Archives and Records Administration, College Park, MD

_____. Regarding movement orders, dated October 23, 1945, NARA RG 389, Entry 261, Box 2563. National Archives and Records Administration, College Park, MD

_____. Regarding movement orders, dated September 18, 1945, NARA RG 389, Entry 261, Box 2563. National Archives and Records Administration, College Park, MD

Wardlow, Chester. *United States Army in World War II: The Technical Services: The Transportation Corps: Movements, Training, and Supply.* Center of Military History, United States Army, Washington, DC, 2003.

Washington, Death Certificates, 1907–1960, index, FamilySearch (familysearch.org/pal:/MM9.1.1/N3T1-ZR2), Biambick Burbien, September 28, 1945.

_____. Death Certificates, 1907–1960, index, FamilySearch (familysearch.org/pal:/MM9.1.1/N3T1-8V1), Vincenzo Dioguardi, December 22, 1945.

_____. Death Certificates, 1907–1960, index, FamilySearch (familysearch.org/pal:/MM9.1.1/N3T1-ZXQ), Elisabar Elisbaraschwili, August 6, 1945.

_____. Death Certificates, 1907–1960, index, FamilySearch (familysearch.org/pal:/MM9.1.1/N3TB-S8C), Albert Marquardt, October 1, 1945.

_____. Death Certificates, 1907–1960, index, FamilySearch (familysearch.org/pal:/MM9.1.1/N3TR-K91), Kurt Messner, August 18, 1945.

_____. Death Certificates, 1907–1960, index, FamilySearch (familysearch.org/pal:/MM9.1.1/N3TG-N12), Gughielmo Olivotta, August 14, 1944.

_____. Death Certificates, 1907–1960, index, FamilySearch (familysearch.org/pal:/MM9.1.1/N3TT-QHC), Leo Paluczkiewicz, July 4, 1945.

_____. Death Certificates, 1907–1960, index, FamilySearch (familysearch.org/pal:/MM9.1.1/N3TR-FXP), Karl Simon, January 20, 1945.

Weyand, A.M., Col. Commanding, Prisoner of War Camp, Ogden, UT, Letter regarding prisoner segregation, dated January 21, 1944, NARA RG 389, Entry 261, Box 2563. National Archives and Records Administration, College Park, MD

Whittingham, Richard. *Martial Justice: the Last Mass Execution in the United States.* Bluejacket Books, Naval Institute Press, Annapolis, MD. 1997

Wilcox, Walter W. "The Wartime Use of Manpower on Farms." Journal of Farm Economics 28, No. 3 (Aug. 1946): 723–741.

Winter, Richard. "Hot Springs, NC. A World War I Internment Camp." *North Carolina Postal Historian* 27, no. 1 (2008)

"WWI German Prisoners of War in Utah," GenTracer, gentracer.org/WWIGermanPrisonersofWarinUtah.html.

"WWI Internment Camp in Hot Springs, NC: The German Village," Welcome to Madison County, North Carolina, visitmadisoncounty.com/who-we-are/town-of-hot-springs/the-german-village-wwi-internment-camp/.

Acknowledgments

Christine Saffell (researcher and travel companion)
Kate and John Saffell (website, data entry, photos)
Alessandro de Gaetano (producer, screenwriter of Red Gold)
Andrea Boni and family (son of Guido Boni, an Italian POW)
Andrea Selmi and family (son of Carlo Selmi, an Italian POW)
Barbara Harvey (Mother, support, great memory for events in her lifetime)
Carmelina Impellizzeri (daughter of Vincenzo Lo Giudice, an Italian POW)
Carol A. Jensen (historian and author)
Dave Kendziura (historian, Hill AFB)
Gina McNeeley (photographic expert, NARA researcher)
Jinger La Guardia (colleague who shares the goal of saving these "lost" stories)
Karen Jensen and Pam Frisbie (my sisters who share the lure of the stories behind the headstones)
Karrie and Jenefer Jackson (data entry)
Kenneth D. Schlessinger (NARA II, College Park, MD)
Kent Powell (Utah Historical Society)
Marcello Turrini (son of Mario Turrini, an Italian POW)
Col. Maurizio Parri (grandson of General Dino Parri, an Italian POW)
Michael Luick-Thrams (TRACES founder)
Michael Pomeroy (authority on Camp Monticello, AR)
Orazio and Giovanni Vecchio (son/nephew and grandson of Orazio and Angelo Vecchio, Italian POW brothers)
Rhonda Jackson and Lucia Rogers (researchers)
Sarah Langsdon (Special Collections, Weber State University)
Stefano Palermo (son of Raffaele Palermo an Italian POW)

Please contact the author at gentracer@gmail.com to share your knowledge about the prisoners of war stories, photos, letters, and artifacts that may be part of your family and local history.

Index